Twentieth-Century Pittsburgh

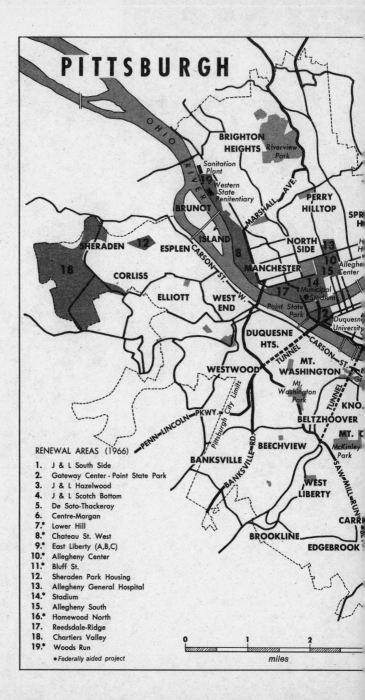

PITTSBURGH

BRIGHTON HEIGHTS

Riverview Park

Sanitation Plant

Western State Penitentiary

BRUNOT

SHERADEN 12

ESPLEN

ISLAND

MARSHALL AVE.

PERRY HILLTOP

SPR H

NORTH SIDE 13

10

15

Alleghe Center

CORLISS

8

MANCHESTER

14

17 *Municipal Stadium*

ELLIOTT

WEST END

Point State Park

2

Duquesne University

DUQUESNE HTS.

WESTWOOD

MT. WASHINGTON

Mt. Washington Park

TUNNEL

CARSON ST.

KNO.

BANKSVILLE

BELTZHOOVER

MT. C

McKinley Park

BEECHVIEW

PENN-LINCOLN PKWY.

Pittsburgh City Limits

BANKSVILLE RD.

SAW MILL RUN R.

WEST LIBERTY

CARR

BROOKLINE

EDGEBROOK

RENEWAL AREAS (1966)

1. J & L South Side
2. Gateway Center - Point State Park
3. J & L Hazelwood
4. J & L Scotch Bottom
5. De Soto-Thackeray
6. Centre-Morgan
7.* Lower Hill
8.* Chateau St. West
9.* East Liberty (A,B,C)
10.* Allegheny Center
11.* Bluff St.
12. Sheraden Park Housing
13. Allegheny General Hospital
14.* Stadium
15. Allegheny South
16.* Homewood North
17. Reedsdale-Ridge
18. Chartiers Valley
19.* Woods Run

*Federally aided project

0   1   2

miles

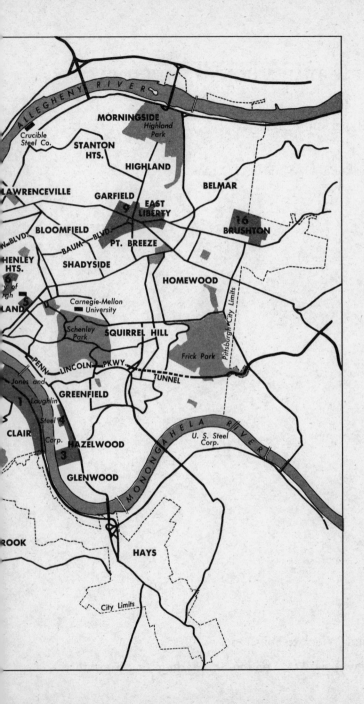

NEW DIMENSIONS IN HISTORY

Historical Cities

Series Editor: Norman F. Cantor

John Wiley & Sons, Inc.,
New York · London · Sydney · Toronto

TWENTIETH-CENTURY PITTSBURGH

Government, Business, and Environmental Change

ROY LUBOVE

University of Pittsburgh

PREFACE

This study deals with the process of environmental change in twentieth-century Pittsburgh. The Pittsburgh experience suggests how misleading it is to interpret urban reform historically in terms of an uprising against "business." On the contrary, the business and professional leadership of Pittsburgh, operating often through voluntary civic organizations, initiated and dominated the environmental reform tradition. Second, the Pittsburgh experience clarifies the advantages and limitations of a reform process sustained by a business and professional elite. The main advantage, as the post-World War II Pittsburgh "Renaissance" suggests, is the capacity for decisive action once a consensus on objectives is reached; the limitation is that issues are defined and programs established largely in response to business objectives. Finally, the Pittsburgh experience suggests that the 1960's witnessed the emergence of a new, neighborhood-centered challenge to elite hegemony. Corporate influence remained dominant in determining what would or would not be done in Pittsburgh, but neighborhood groups were now demanding a significant voice in the decision-making process.

I have accumulated numerous debts in the course of preparing this book. The staffs of the University of Pittsburgh and the Carnegie Libraries were invariably helpful. The Pennsylvania Division of the Carnegie Library was an especially valuable resource. Assistance was rendered by several members of the faculty of the Graduate School of Social Work, University of Pittsburgh: Morton Coleman, James V. Cunningham, Meyer Schwartz, and Kiernan Stenson. Participants in some of the events described, all four provided information and encouragement. I am indebted also to Dean William H. McCullough and the Graduate School of Social Work for creating a favorable atmosphere for research. Bernard E. Loshbough, director of ACTION-

Housing, read and criticized a draft of Chapter Seven; B. Burtt Evans, director of information and publications, ACTION-Housing, also looked over this material. The author alone is responsible for any errors of fact or interpretation.

Joseph Verwer assisted the author in using the Buhl Foundation Archives. Regrettably, not all Pittsburgh agencies—public and private—are as conscientious as the Buhl Foundation in maintaining records. Much valuable historical material has already been destroyed by the Chamber of Commerce, Department of City Planning, and ACTION-Housing—to name just a few leading offenders. ACTION-Housing, on the other hand, is to be commended for its fairly systematic publication and distribution of reports. Social and governmental agencies in Pittsburgh tend to be rather informal about this—either preparing no reports or consigning requests for material to some special limbo. I hope that this book will encourage the Pittsburgh social and planning agencies to consign their records to a library instead of the sanitation department.

To conclude on a more cheerful note, Christine Biedinger's secretarial contributions were, as always, exemplary.

ROY LUBOVE

CONTENTS

LIST OF MAPS

MAPS BY JOHN V. MORRIS

LIST OF ILLUSTRATIONS

Twentieth-Century Pittsburgh

ONE

The Balance of Life and Work

Pittsburgh, the "Renaissance" and "Cinderella" city of urban renewal after World War II, projected a more squalid image throughout most of its history. It was the "Smoky City," America's classic Coketown. Few communities were so frequently compared to hell. A visitor in the 1880's felt as though he had "reached the outer edge of the infernal regions. . . . One pictures, as he beholds it, the tortured spirits writhing in agony, their sinewy limbs convulsed, and the very air oppressive with pain and rage." And Lincoln Steffens never forgot his first impression: "It looked like hell, literally."[1]

Social critics, by the early twentieth century, likened Pittsburgh to a human as well as a physical "inferno." Labor conditions were "horrifying"; men were treated as "cogs" and "animals." The journalist Samuel Hopkins Adams, after an investigation of the city's health problems, arrived at the morbid conclusion that the infant mortality rate was too low. It might be better, he reflected, "for the unfortunate and innocent victims themselves, and certainly for the community at large, that this puny, helpless breed of hunger, filth, and misery which creeps about the city's manmade jungles, should succumb in infancy to the conditions that bred but cannot support them."[2]

[1] Willard Glazier, *Peculiarities of American Cities* (Philadelphia: Hubbard Brothers, 1885), 332, 333; *The Autobiography of Lincoln Steffens* (New York: Harcourt, Brace and Company, 1931), 401.
[2] "In the Interpreter's House," *American Magazine,* 69 (September 1909), 518; James Oppenheim, "The Hired City," *American Magazine,* 70 (May 1910), 38; Samuel Hopkins Adams, "Pittsburgh's Foregone Asset, the Public Health: A Running Summary of the Present Administrative Situation," *Charities and the Commons,* 21 (February 6, 1909), 945.

Pittsburgh was a symbol as well as a city. It was synonymous with the spectacular advance of American industry, and the byproducts: labor unrest, poverty, assimilation of a heterogeneous immigrant working force, and disruption of community cohesion. Pittsburgh was also the symbol for a broader metropolitan and regional complex whose one unifying force was business enterprise. Whether conceived as city, district, or region, Pittsburgh was an economic rather than a civic entity. Economic rationalization existed in a context of governmental and social fragmentation. In America's representative industrial center, both physical environment and social institutions were shaped by a relentless economic discipline.

The city of Pittsburgh sprawled out in all directions from the confluence of the Allegheny and Monongahela Rivers. East of the Point, where the rivers joined, was Pittsburgh's cramped central business district. The Ohio River flowed westward past Pittsburgh's North Side (Allegheny City before 1907) and West End. Most of the flatland fronting on all three rivers was preempted by industrial and commercial enterprises. The desecration of a superb natural environment—one of America's most spectacular in its combination of water-breaks, topography, and verdure—was total. "Man befouled the streams, bedraggled their banks, ripped up the cliffs, hacked down the trees, and dumped refuse in their stead. He sowed the imposing heights with hovels and set beneath them black mills to cover everything far and wide with a film of smoke."[3]

The metropolis had some redeeming features. There were the giant Schenley, Highland, and Riverview Parks and the fascinations of the river scene. Spacious mansions and homes dotted the suburban East End. H. H. Richardson's downtown county courthouse and jail had enriched America's architectural heritage since the 1880's. It sparked a Romanesque revival well suited to the elephantine stone and brick architecture favored by Pittsburghers.[4] The city also possessed an elaborate "Civic Center"

[3] Robert Haven Schauffler, *Romantic America* (New York: Century Company, 1913), 71.
[4] On Richardson and the Romanesque, see James D. Van Trump, "The Romanesque Revival in Pittsburgh," *Journal of the Society of Architectural Historians,* **16** (October 1957), 22–28.

in its Oakland district adjoining Schenley Park. Here was the showplace of Pittsburgh culture, and an enduring testimony to the follies of the City Beautiful movement that had been inspired by the Chicago Fair of 1893. The Civic Center became the "cosmetic," as Mumford termed it, applied to the ugly sores of the nineteenth century industrial city.[5]

As one left the city and penetrated the hinterland, visual or cultural amenities became scarce. Allegheny County, roughly coterminous with the Pittsburgh industrial district, contained a population of little over 1 million in 1910. Of these, 271,000 were foreign-born, and another 342,000 were the children of foreign-born. A procession of mill towns lined the rivers, especially the barge-laden Monongahela, drab and muddy as the atmosphere of the coal and steel communities it passed on route to Morgantown, West Virginia. Surrounding Allegheny were the five other counties that comprised the Pittsburgh region: Armstrong, Beaver, Butler, Washington, and Westmoreland. The 4500 square miles of the Pittsburgh region claimed a population of 1.6 million in 1910 (534,000 of whom resided in the city of Pittsburgh).[6]

[5] The Oakland civic center area, then known as the Schenley Farms district, included the Carnegie Institute (library, museum, and music hall); Carnegie Technical Schools (Carnegie Institute of Technology); University of Pittsburgh; Rodef Sholem Synagogue; Soldiers' and Sailors' Memorial; Pittsburgh Athletic Club; Masonic Hall; University Club; Colonial Club; Twentieth Century Club; Historical Society of Western Pennsylvania; Forbes Field; Schenley Hotel; First Congregational Church; First Baptist Church; and Calvary Church. Many of the buildings were designed by two firms: Palmer, Hornbostel, and Jones; and Janssen and Abbott. See Aymar Embury II, "Impressions of Three Cities, III, Pittsburgh," *Architecture*, 31 (April 1915), 105–09; and Montgomery Schuyler, "The Building of Pittsburgh," *Architectural Record*, 30 (September 1911), 229 ff.

[6] Bertram J. Black and Aubrey Mallach, *Population Trends in Allegheny County, 1840–1943* (Bureau of Social Research, Federation of Social Agencies of Pittsburgh and Allegheny County, April 1944), 2, 4; and *Economic Study of the Pittsburgh Region* (conducted by the Pittsburgh Regional Planning Association), Vol. II, *Portrait of a Region*, Ira S. Lowry (Pittsburgh: University of Pittsburgh Press, 1963), 37, 39.

The definition of the six-county Pittsburgh region follows the usage of the *Economic Study of the Pittsburgh Region* upon which I have drawn liberally for the following regional economic analysis. The other two volumes are *Region in Transition* and *Region with a Future*, also published in 1963. Although this study does not include Fayette County in the defini-

The regional economy had once been balanced, and included a large agricultural sector. In the quarter century after 1800 Pittsburgh served as a major trade entrepot for markets to the west and south. Ready access to raw materials such as coal and timber soon fostered industrial activity: iron-smelting, metals fabrication, textiles, boat building, and the manufacture of glass-stone-clay products. The locational advantages that had stimulated Pittsburgh's commercial growth diminished with the arrival of the railroad, decline of the river trade, and competition from cities closer to western markets. Uniquely dependent upon locational advantages throughout the nineteenth century, Pittsburgh responded with a maximum exploitation of its competitive superiority in raw materials (notably mineral fuels) needed for heavy industry.

The Pittsburgh region's preeminence in iron and steel production after the 1880's was inseparable from the adoption of coke as the chief iron-smelting fuel. Pittsburgh area manufacturers had ready access to the nearby Connellsville coke fields (Fayette County), whose beehive ovens produced the best metallurgical coke in the United States. As long as coke costs represented the key differential in pig iron (hence steel) costs, no other region could compete. Pittsburgh's hegemony would end only when the semi-monopoly in blast furnace coke was undermined in the twentieth century by the development of by-product coke ovens, which were more economical when situated near the furnaces rather than the mines. This technological innovation facilitated the use of competing coals, and made access to new, rapidly growing markets in the west more important than availability of a single source of coking coal.

The regional economy and community system were fixed in the period 1880–1910, when Connellsville coke established Pittsburgh as the leading iron and steel producer. Coal mining employment grew steadily, reaching a peak of 82,000 by 1914 in the six-county region. The prevalence of cheap fuel, including natural gas, stimulated the growth of the glass industry. Another regional specialty, heavy electrical machinery and transformers, was

tion of the Pittsburgh region, its economic ties with the other counties were close in the early twentieth century.

launched by George Westinghouse; by 1899 the region's proportion of total national employment in electrical manufacturing
was 15.3 percent. By the early twentieth century, the Pittsburgh
region had developed an economic mix that distinguished it from
most other metropolitan areas—an over-specialization in a limited
range of heavy industrial enterprises and a concentration of the
labor force in the large plants associated with its specialties.

Metal production, more than any single factor, shaped the
regional work and community system. The era of steel arrived
when Carnegie opened the Edgar Thomson works at Braddock
in 1875. This was followed by a rapid expansion of steel facilities,
which lasted until 1890. A second period of expansion occurred
between 1900–1903. The opening of the Aliquippa works of
Jones and Laughlin around 1909, and the Midland Works of
Crucible Steel in 1911, marked the last major new plant construction in the region.

Fierce competition in the steel industry until the formation of
the United States Steel Corporation in 1901 profoundly influenced
labor relations. It led, particularly in the Carnegie domain, to a
managerial obsession with cost reduction. One expression of the
drive for economy was technological innovation, which reduced
both costs and the industry's dependence upon skilled labor.
Costs were also controlled by disassociating labor productivity
from wage levels; increased productivity led frequently to reductions in tonnage rates. The ability of the industry to economize
in its labor costs hinged, ultimately, upon the suppression of
unionism. This policy was successfully inaugurated with the de-
feat of the Homestead strikers in 1892. Company power to control
working conditions was reinforced by political influence in the
mill towns and by divisions within the labor force between
skilled and unskilled, American- and foreign-born. The era of
comparatively enlightened, paternalistic management after 1901
was designed primarily to cement the loyalty of the skilled
worker. For the unskilled, foreign labor force, who constituted
the majority, continuity of employment and a degree of mobility
apparently sufficed to insure stability.[7]

[7] See David Brody, *Steelworkers in America: The Nonunion Era* (Cambridge, Mass.: Harvard University Press, 1960).

In this master industry of the Pittsburgh region, the destruction of unionism, company political influence, and ethnic fragmentation produced an enlightened despotism, at best, and a ruthless suppression of dissent, at worst. The ultimate control lay in the use of force, as at Homestead in 1892 and during the great steel strike of 1919, supplemented by an elaborate espionage system to root out malcontents. John Fitch, during his investigations for the Pittsburgh Survey, found that men feared to discuss mill conditions or politics. "I doubt," he explained, "whether you could find a more suspicious body of men than the employes of the United States Steel Corporation. They are suspicious of one another, or their neighbors, and of their friends." At a time when over 500 men a year were killed in the industries of Allegheny County, one worker at the Homestead works assured Fitch that he had never heard of any dangers or seen anybody get hurt. The men believed in the existence of Corporation secret service departments, whose agents were "working shoulder to shoulder at the rolls or furnaces with honest workmen, ready to record any 'disloyal' utterances. . . ."[8]

In the absence of any significant countervailing power, the business leadership was free to shape the life of the region. This had led, by the early twentieth century, to the mutilation and pollution of the physical environment, and to a low priority for housing, health, and social welfare institutions. It was the discrepancy between the level of centralization, coordination, and planning in the economic sector, and the failure to apply similar techniques to environmental and social change, which constituted the main theme of the Pittsburgh Survey of 1907–1908.

The Pittsburgh Survey was not the product of widespread local demand for social criticism and reform. It was engineered by a small group of Pittsburgh business, professional, and welfare leaders in collaboration with the Charities Publication Committee of New York (later Survey Associates). The latter, the official sponsor of the Survey, had undertaken an investigation of social conditions in Washington, D.C. in 1905. Published as a special number of *Charities and the Commons,* the Wash-

[8] John A. Fitch, *The Steel Workers* (New York: Charities Publication Committee, Russell Sage Foundation, 1910), 214, 215, 219.

ington study aroused the interest of Alice B. Montgomery, chief probation officer of the Allegheny Juvenile Court. Her proposal for a similar investigation of Pittsburgh was strongly endorsed by Frank Tucker, a member of the Committee and former journalist. William H. Matthews, headworker at Pittsburgh's Kingsley House settlement, played an important role in lining up local support. Prominent Pittsburghers who consented to serve as references included Mayor George Guthrie, H. D. W. English, president of the Chamber of Commerce, and Judge Joseph Buffington of the United States Circuit Court.[9]

A field staff invaded Pittsburgh in the fall of 1907. It was decided, on the basis of their reports, to expand the scope and depth of the inquiry beyond the "journalistic diagnoses" originally planned; and the newly-organized Russell Sage Foundation granted $27,000 in three installments to finance the project.[10] The main investigations were completed by the spring of 1908, supplemented in 1909 and 1910 by examinations of children's institutions, taxation, and labor law administration. In November, 1908 a graphic exhibit was held at the Carnegie Institute.[11] Survey findings were published in three successive monthly is-

[9] Paul U. Kellogg, "The Social Engineer in Pittsburgh," *New Outlook*, 93 (September 25, 1909), 165–66; and Paul U. Kellogg, "Field Work of the Pittsburgh Survey," in *The Pittsburgh District: Civic Frontage* (New York: Survey Associates, Russell Sage Foundation, 1914), 492–515.

[10] The Survey was launched with a contribution of $1000 from the Charities Publication Committee, supplemented by the following sums from Pittsburgh sources: Civic Club, $50; H. J. Heinz, $100; Wallace H. Rowe, $100; Benjamin Thaw, $50; and Mrs. William R. Thompson, $50. The first Russell Sage grant of $7000 was allocated in the spring of 1907. *Ibid.*, 497–498; John M. Glenn, et al., *Russell Sage Foundation, 1907–1946* (New York: Russell Sage Foundation, 1947), I, 211.

[11] Paul U. Kellogg, "The New Campaign for Civic Betterment: The Pittsburgh Survey of Social and Economic Conditions," *Review of Reviews*, 39 (January 1909), 77–81. The Exhibit was the first general one on social conditions and was based upon specialized precedents like the Tenement House Exhibition of the New York Charity Organization Society in 1900. It was sponsored by a local Citizens' Reception and Entertainment Committee, headed by Oliver McClintock and organized by Benjamin C. Marsh, secretary of the New York Committee on Congestion of Population. The Exhibit included material on typhoid fever and pure water, model company housing, the composition of the labor force, stogy manufacture, and Homestead.

sues of *Charities and the Commons,* beginning in January, 1909, followed by six summary volumes (1909–1914).[12]

The Pittsburgh Survey was a unique experiment in American social and community analysis. Never before had so many specialists been drawn together to explore so many facets of a community's life. The field staff and contributors to the published reports constituted an honor roll of authorities in social welfare and social investigation. The Survey was equally distinctive in its effort to explore a wide range of social, industrial, and civic issues, and relate them to each other. It differed, in this respect, from earlier but more limited investigations of housing, health, cost of living, or vice in American cities. Third, the Survey, focusing upon the wage-earning population, attempted to "reduce conditions to terms of household experience and human life," to put institutions to the "test of a distinctively human measure."[13] It achieved, in this connection, an impressive synthesis between the statistical, empirical perspective of the census report, and the vivid, personalized touch of the journalist.

[12] Elizabeth Beardsley Butler, *Women and the Trades, Pittsburgh, 1907–1908* (New York: Charities Publication Committee, Russell Sage Foundation, 1909); Margaret F. Byington, *Homestead: The Households of a Mill Town* (New York: Charities Publication Committee, Russell Sage Foundation, 1910); Crystal Eastman, *Work-Accidents and the Law* (New York: Survey Associates, Russell Sage Foundation, 1910); Fitch, *The Steel Workers; The Pittsburgh District: Civic Frontage; Wage-Earning Pittsburgh* (New York: Survey Associates, Russell Sage Foundation, 1911).

The Pittsburgh Survey led, in 1912, to the establishment of a Department of Surveys and Exhibits in the Russell Sage Foundation. After a few years, survey technique shifted from appraisals of general conditions to specialized investigations such as that conducted by Leonard P. Ayres on education in Cleveland. On the origins and development of the survey idea, see Paul U. Kellogg, "Our Hidden Cities: And the American Zest for Discovery," *Survey,* 60 (July 1, 1928), 391–392, 409–411, 416; Paul U. Kellogg and Neva R. Deardorff, "Social Research as Applied to Community Progress," First International Conference of Social Work, *Proceedings* (1928), I, 784–831; Shelby M. Harrison, *The Social Survey: The Idea Defined and its Development Traced* (New York: Russell Sage Foundation, 1931).

[13] Paul U. Kellogg, "The Spread of the Survey Idea," New York Academy of Political Science, *Proceedings* (1911–1912), 476; "The Pittsburgh Survey: Of the National Publication Committee of Charities and the Commons," *Charities and the Commons,* 19 (March 7, 1908), 1667.

Finally, the Pittsburgh Survey was notable for its action orientation. The findings were too timely, the issues too pressing, to await publication in book form. As the studies proceeded, they were interpreted through "luncheon meetings, newspapers, magazine articles, pamphlets, addresses, exhibits."[14] And the Survey attempted to stimulate and link up with local reform efforts in health, housing, taxation, charity organization, and other fields.

Paul U. Kellogg, editor of the Survey, and his colleagues emphasized that Pittsburgh had not been singled out as some monstrous aberration among American communities. To the contrary, they stressed the city's representative qualities; their effort would not have been worthwhile if it had merely local significance. This was the whole point of the endeavor, despite misunderstanding by native Pittsburghers who reacted with "feelings of mingled humiliation and indignation" because they were "held up as a money grasping people, with little of the milk of human kindness." Pittsburgh, Kellogg insisted, "is not merely a scapegoat city. It is the capital of a district representative of untrammeled industrial development, but of a district which, for richer, for poorer, in sickness and in health, for vigor, waste and optimism, is rampantly American."[15]

Edward Devine of the New York Charity Organization Society summarized the indictment against the "rampantly American" city of Pittsburgh. Nothing disturbed the authors of the Survey more than the "incredible amount of overwork by everybody, reaching its extreme in the twelve-hour shift for seven days in the week in the steel mills and the railway switchyards." Wages, for the majority of mill workers, were not commensurate with the hours or strenuous physical demands; they were adjusted to the single man rather than the family, and they were low in relation to prices. Pittsburgh suffered from an absentee capitalism and landlordism that undermined civic cohesion. Confronted with overwhelming problems of social and environmental pathol-

[14] Kellogg, "Field Work of the Pittsburgh Survey," 501 (cited in footnote 9).
[15] Pittsburgh Association for the Improvement of the Poor, *Thirty-Eighth Annual Report, 1913–1914*, 5; Paul U. Kellogg, "The Pittsburgh Survey," *Charities and the Commons*, 21 (January 2, 1909), 525.

ogy, Pittsburgh abounded in "archaic social institutions" and "unregenerate" charities.[16]

It added up to an imbalance of life and work. No community in history had ever generated such "prosperity" and "surplus" from its production machinery, but "never before has a great community applied what it had so meagerly to the rational purposes of human life." Workers in the "master industry" were "driven as large numbers of laborers whether slave or free have scarcely before in human history been driven." The imbalance of life and work had become lethal, resulting in the "destruction of family life, not in any imaginary or mystical sense, but by the demands of the day's work, and by the very demonstrable and material method of typhoid fever and industrial accidents."[17]

Paul Kellogg interpreted the Survey as an "appraisal, if you will, of how far human engineering had kept pace with mechanical in the American steel district." The Survey demonstrated, if anything, that "democracy must overhaul the social machinery through which it operates if it would bring its community conditions up to standards comparable to those maintained by its banks, its insurance companies and its industrial corporations." We needed a "social hydraulics" that would insure the continuous adaptation of "old social institutions and usages" to "changing tides." Efficiency through centralization and planning were required for social as well as business institutions. Thus the crucial contrast in Pittsburgh lay between the "haphazard development of its social institutions [and] the splendid organic development of its business enterprises." All the "progressiveness and invention" had gone into Pittsburgh the industrial center, and not Pittsburgh the community. One had only to compare the efficiency of the blast furnace in performing its function with the efficiency of many of the houses in performing theirs.[18]

Wherever they looked, the authors of the Survey found a

---

[16] Edward T. Devine, "Results of the Pittsburgh Survey," *American Journal of Sociology*, 14 (March 1909), 661, 662.

[17] *Ibid.*, 662, 664.

[18] Kellogg, "Our Hidden Cities," 392; Paul U. Kellogg, "The Civic Responsibilities of Democracy in an Industrial District," Conference for Good City Government, *Proceedings* (1908), 399–400, 394, 398, 403; Kellogg, "The Pittsburgh Survey," 524.

startling contrast between the dynamic, planned industrial sector, and the bumbling, archaic mix of governmental and civic institutions that failed, literally, to safeguard human life. Crystal Eastman documented this point in her study of work injuries. She revealed that 526 men were killed by work accidents in Allegheny County alone between July 1, 1906 and June 30, 1907. Most were under 40 years of age. Responsibility for the accidents was often attributable to circumstances beyond the worker's control, yet the survivors usually received little or no compensation from employers. On the grounds of equity and social expediency, she urged the enactment of a workmen's compensation law to prevent destitution and penalize the careless employer. Meanwhile, considering the human and economic repercussions of industrial accidents, it was "no wonder that to a stranger Pittsburgh's streets are sad."[19]

Elizabeth Butler explored the status of working women. She found, in the winter of 1907–1908, a total of 22,185 female wage earners (exclusive of agriculture, domestic service, and the professions). Over a third (7540) were employed in mercantile houses, followed by food production (2726), laundries (2685), and stogy manufacture (2611). Many of these women, she observed, "are put to work at wages below the cost of subsistence, for hours longer than the measure of their strength, in buildings and at ill-constructed machines which cannot but injure their health, and at processes which must handicap heavily the development of both body and mind."[20] More than 60 percent of the women earned less than $7 a week, the sum considered to be the subsistence minimum for a self-supporting working girl.

John Fitch examined the steel industry, whose work force in Allegheny County totaled 70,000 to 80,000. This was the prime exhibit of the imbalance of life and work, of economic rationalism in a context of social and community fragmentation. The organization of the United States Steel Corporation in 1901 placed 50 percent of the nation's steel workers under a single employer, "with a resulting promotion of uniformity of conditions of labor. Administrative decisions from a single head affect, without

[19] Eastman, *Work-Accidents and the Law*, 13 (cited in footnote 12).
[20] Butler, *Women and the Trades*, 28 (cited in footnote 12).

chance of protest, vast masses of men." Isolated individuals confronted an impersonal economic machine, and the "steel worker
sees on every side evidences of an irresistible power, baffling
and intangible." Neither church nor town exerted any countervailing influence "through which democratic action and ideals
may find expression and conditions be improved."[21] The orientation of the churches was individualistic and moralistic. The
sanctity of the Sabbath (as far as amusement was concerned),
vice, and liquor absorbed the attention of the clergy. Except in
McKeesport, where authority was shared with the brewing interests, the steel companies were "commonly understood" to be
the dominant political force. Social alignments in the mill towns
"also buttressed the dominance of management." Merchants and
professional men "recognized a kinship with the plant officialdom," while the English-speaking worker identified more with
the town middle class than with the despised "Hunky."[22]

The isolation and powerlessness of the steel worker would be
starkly dramatized in the strike of 1919, when the normal pattern
of stability and control broke down as a result of World War I.
The interlocking of plant and town officialdom explained "not
only the ease with which normal civil rights have been shelved,
but the ease with which, under the guise of law enforcement,
deputies and troopers get away with reckless action in the streets
and alleys, and with which the petty courts turn trumped-up
grounds for the arrest of labor organizers and strikers into de-
nials of justice." In denying a permit to union organizers for a
meeting, Mayor Crawford of Duquesne reputedly stated that
"'Jesus Christ himself couldn't hold a meeting in Duquesne.'"[23]

[21] Fitch, *The Steel Workers*, 5, 232, 223 (cited in footnote 12).
[22] *Ibid.*, 229; Brody, *Steelworkers in America*, 118, 121 (cited in footnote 7).
[23] S. Adele Shaw, "Closed Towns: Intimidation as it is Practiced in the
Pittsburgh Steel District," *Survey*, 43 (November 8, 1919), 64, 62. For
John Fitch, events in the Pittsburgh steel district in 1919 ran "true to form.
Unionism was destroyed there in 1892. Since then every manifestation of an
independent spirit on the part of the workers has been met by ruthless and
unscrupulous opposition." John A. Fitch, "Democracy in Steel: A Contrast
between the Rhine and the Monongahela," *Survey*, 41 (January 4, 1919),
453. Charges of repression and other events surrounding the strike of 1919
are examined in Interchurch World Movement, The Commission of Inquiry,

The Mayor was president of the First National Bank of Duquesne, and his brother was president of the McKeesport Tin Plate Company. Years earlier, Fitch concluded that the worker in quest for democracy and solidarity had nowhere to turn except his saloon and fraternal lodge.

Politics, health, and housing suffered in the eyes of the Pittsburgh Survey investigators, when economic cohesion confronted class, ethnic, and governmental fragmentation. This militated against a mobilization of resources in the civic sector comparable to that in the economic sector. Pittsburgh's ward-centered political, school, and tax systems before 1911 were symptomatic of the "organic problem of American cities generally"—a "neighborhood instead of municipal spirit" that gave free reign to parochial interests. The absence of any "communal interests" helped explain why it was so difficult to apply the "economy of organization to the common uses of the people."[24]

The "economy of organization" was urgent in public health and housing. Typhoid fever was endemic in the decade preceding the establishment of a water filtration plant in 1907. The Pittsburgh and Allegheny typhoid death rate of 130.0 and 104.4 per 100,000, respectively, were the highest in the nation.[25] Skunk Hollow and Painter's Row were characteristic of the housing of a community in which the industrial sector alone was expertly administered and capable of decisive action, yet indifferent to

Report on the Steel Strike of 1919 (New York: Harcourt, Brace and Company, 1920), and Interchurch World Movement, *Public Opinion and the Steel Strike. Supplementary Reports of the Investigators to the Commission of Inquiry* (New York: Harcourt, Brace and Company, 1921). A recent study is David Brody, *Labor in Crisis: The Steel Strike of 1919* (Philadelphia and New York: J. P. Lippincott Company, 1965).

[24] Allen T. Burns, "Coalition of Pittsburgh's Civic Forces," in *The Pittsburgh District: Civic Frontage,* 47; Paul U. Kellogg, "Pittsburgh: Community and Workshop," in *Wage-Earning Pittsburgh,* 5.

[25] Frank E. Wing, "Thirty-Five Years of Typhoid: The Economic Cost to Pittsburgh and the Long Fight for Pure Water," in the *Pittsburgh District: Civic Frontage,* 66. The first filtered water was pumped into the Highland Reservoir in December, 1907. By the end of 1908, the city's water supply, except for the South Side, was filtered. Filtered water for the South Side followed in 1909. See Commonwealth of Pennsylvania, Department of Health, *Report on the Sanitary Survey of the Allegheny River Basin* (Harrisburg, 1915), 314.

any aspect of civic life that had no bearing on production efficiency. Ewing Street ran along the edge of Skunk Hollow, close by the Bloomfield Bridge. So fantastic was the dilapidation here that it was difficult to tell whether the shacks were supposed to accommodate humans or animals. Official condemnation would be superfluous since the dwellings were already falling apart. The contents of outside privies seeped down the slope to the rubbish-laden Hollow. Painter's Row, on the South Side, belonged to the U. S. Steel Corporation. It had inherited the property from the Carnegie Company which, in turn, had absorbed Painter's Mill. Although the Carnegie firm had renovated the plant, it did nothing for the 91 families who inhabited the six rows of brick and frame homes. Five hundred persons lived in these "back-to-back houses with no through ventilation; cellar kitchens; dark, unsanitary, ill-ventilated, overcrowded sleeping rooms, no drinking water supply on the premises; and a dearth of sanitary accommodations that was shameful."[26] An old pump in the mill yard was the sole source of drinking water.

Margaret Byington devoted considerable attention to housing in her portrait of Homestead, a classic account of a milltown spawned in the nineteenth century. Byington's Homestead was the Pittsburgh region in microcosm—a case study in industrial cohesion and community fragmentation. The mill masters, she complained, did not consider living conditions as a factor of production, but there was no alternative group or institution with the power to intervene effectively in the environment. Homestead's physical environment, family life, and social institutions were the product of "indifference on one side," paralysis and "ignorance" on the other.[27]

Originally established as a residential suburb of Pittsburgh in the 1870's, Homestead's industrial phase opened with a glass factory in 1878 and a steel mill in 1881 (later absorbed into the Carnegie empire). The protracted, bloody strike in the Homestead steel works in 1892 precipitated the destruction of unionism

[26] F. Elisabeth Crowell, "Three Studies in Housing and Responsibility, 2. Painter's Row, The Company House," in *The Pittsburgh District: Civic Frontage*, 130.
[27] Margaret F. Byington, "The Family in a Typical Mill Town," *American Journal of Sociology*, 14 (March 1909), 655.

in the Pittsburgh steel industry, and insured that the worker would have little share in determining "his hours, his wages, and the conditions under which he works,—and which in turn vitally affect the well-being of his family."[28]

According to the census of 1900, native whites of native white parents were already a minority of 36 percent of the population. Fifty-three percent of the men employed in the mill in 1907 were of Slavic origin. As in other milltowns, there was a large number of unmarried transient males, particularly among the immigrants; and the corps of young college graduates employed in the mill added to the transient population. English- and foreign-speaking groups led parallel lives with virtually no social intercourse. Class stratification reinforced the separation and contributed to the breakdown of community cohesion. Absentee ownership was another factor that undermined Homestead as a civic entity.

Political and topographical fragmentation also limited the community's ability to define and cope with its problems. The original steel works were situated in Homestead Borough, a small triangle whose base touched the Monongahela River. Mill expansion along the riverfront stimulated additional settlement to the east and west of Homestead. This led, not to the enlargement of the borough's boundaries, but to the creation of two new boroughs—Munhall to the east and West Homestead. Each of these autonomous jurisdictions had its own set of officials, ordinances, and tax levies. Although Homestead had the largest population and concentration of low-paid workers, most of the mill property was located in Munhall, whose borough and school taxes were little more than half the rate in Homestead. Since assessors tended to value smaller properties at the highest rates, the large industries contributed a disproportionately small share of taxes. In contrast to the industrial sector, the civic sector was hopelessly atomized.

Homestead's water supply was drawn from the Monongahela, polluted by sewerage from numerous towns and villages as well as industrial wastes and acid discharges from mines. Individuals sunk wells, but these were frequently contaminated by seepage from privy vaults. No business corporation, certainly, would have

---

[28] Byington, *Homestead*, 11 (cited in footnote 12).

allowed its production facilities to be developed in the sporadic, planless manner of the health and housing environment. Beyond Munhall, for example, was the Hollow, a "deep ravine with a meandering stream at the bottom and with irregular rows of houses, often hardly more than shanties, on either hand."[29] No streets led to the 250 small frame boxes in which unskilled mill workers resided. An intensive study of 21 courts in Homestead's second ward portrayed a characteristic housing style in the Pittsburgh area. These courts accommodated 239 families (102 of whom took lodgers) sharing yard, toilet, and water facilities. Only three houses had indoor running water, and in some cases, more than 100 persons depended on one yard hydrant. There was not a single indoor toilet in any of the courts. Some houses were four to six stories high, but the majority were two stories with four rooms, and all suffered from an absence of light and ventilation.

In Homestead, and elsewhere in the Pittsburgh region, family and town confronted the mill—the "new, insurgent" force, as Kellogg described it. The confrontation led to a disequilibrium in the "balance of life and work" and to a bitter irony. Homestead received a library from Carnegie, a manual traning school from Schwab, and a "charming little park in the centre of the hill section" from Frick. One witnessed the spectacle of a philanthropy that "provides opportunities for intellectual and social advancement while it withholds conditions which make it possible to take advantage of them."[30]

Another philanthropy found in Homestead and other mill and mining communities was company housing. The Carnegie Land Company, following the Homestead strike, had acquired property later incorporated into Munhall. It built and sold a number of homes to employees and retained others for rental. Company housing, however, was not as extensive in the Pittsburgh district as in other parts of the country.[31] It was most prevalent in iso-

[29] *Ibid.*, 18.
[30] *Ibid.*, v, 178.
[31] The greatest proportion of the labor supply, 71 percent, was housed by southern cotton mill owners, followed by soft-coal operators at 61 percent. Preference, in most cases, was given to skilled workers. Leifur Magnusson,

lated or temporary communities and was more characteristic of the mining than the steel industry in the relatively urbanized Pittsburgh area. In a few cases the establishment of a major steel plant, such as Jones and Laughlin at Aliquippa in 1909, and Crucible Steel at Midland in 1911, led not only to company housing but extensive town development as well.[32]

Vandergrift was a rare, often cited example in the Pittsburgh region of an effort to coordinate industrial planning with high standards of town planning. It was the Pullman of western Pennsylvania, self-consciously conceived as a model community that would demonstrate that men lived up to their environment (and that a good environment would produce respectable citizens and a stable labor force). Nestled in the Kiskiminetas River valley in Armstrong County, forty miles east of Pittsburgh, Vandergrift was established by George McMurtry in the 1890's. President of the Apollo Iron and Steel Company (later American Sheet and Tin Plate Company), McMurtry apparently was not fazed by the disastrous climax of Pullman's experiment in community planning. He was determined to prove anew that men, "given an opportunity to live in a clean, healthy, beautiful town," would become model citizens.[33] He studied precedents in Europe and the United States, and hired Frederick Law Olmsted as his planner. Most visitors to Vandergrift were favorably impressed.

"Employers' Housing in the United States," United States Department of Labor, Bureau of Labor Statistics, *Monthly Review*, V (November 1917), 44. More extensive treatment of the subject appears in Leifur Magnusson, "Housing by Employers in the United States," United States Department of Labor, Bureau of Labor Statistics, *Bulletin*, Miscellaneous Series, No. 263 (Washington, D.C., 1920).

[32] John Ihlder, "Midland," *Survey*, 33 (December 12, 1914), 300; Albert H. Spahr, "The Town of Midland, Pa.: A New Development in Housing near Pittsburgh," *Architectural Review*, 21 (N.S.4) (March 1916), 33–36; *Boot Straps: The Autobiography of Tom M. Girdler*, in collaboration with Boyden Sparkes (New York: C. Scribner's Sons, 1943), 169 ff.; Agnes W. Mitchell, "The Industrial Backgrounds and Community Problems of a Large Steel Plant (The Jones and Laughlin Steel Corporation, Aliquippa, Pa.)," unpublished M. A., University of Pittsburgh, 1932, 17 ff.

[33] Ida M. Tarbell, *New Ideals in Business: An Account of Their Practice and Their Effects Upon Men and Profits* (New York: Macmillan Company, 1916), 154.

In Ida Tarbell's opinion, "it would be difficult in the United States to-day to find a prettier town, greener, trimmer, cleaner, and more influential."[34]

More typical of the company town were the "ghastly" communities established for bituminous coal and coke miners. The problem was not the individual house but indifference to the broader environment. One village was like another for the immigrant Slavs who constituted a majority of the labor force in the bituminous mining country by the early twentieth century. Regular rows of 50 to 100 box-like, two-story frame dwellings spanned the hillsides. At one end of the village was the company store and at the other a schoolhouse or church. Below, enveloped in the valley smog, were the engine house and coal tipple. Along the valley floor were the coke ovens, spewing flames and a thick, dirty smoke that the wind lofted up to the village. Sometimes, not a "spear of grass" survived the pollution. The coal companies did not bother with sanitation and other improvements, claiming that the "foreigner is too dirty for the town to be other than what it is." Gutters, ditches, and gulleys collected refuse, and the sidewalks often consisted of coke ash. Surface drainage and privy vaults near the houses were characteristic sanitary expedients.[35]

Sanitary conditions in the city of Pittsburgh were not much better. Before the turn of the century, the Metropolis, like the meanest mining village, exerted few controls over the physical environment. A limited conception of municipal service and welfare functions had prevailed through the nineteenth century.

[34] *Ibid.*, 151. Unskilled workers were later accommodated by the company in an adjoining development, Vandergrift Heights. Others settled in East Vandergrift. The model town is also described in Eugene J. Buffington, "Making Cities for Workmen," *Harper's Weekly*, **53** (May 9, 1909), 16.

[35] This portrait of the coal village is drawn from Reports of the Immigration Commission, *Immigrants in Industries (in twenty-five parts)*, Part 1: Bituminous Coal Mining (in two volumes), Vol. 1, 61st Cong., 2nd sess., Senate, Doc. No. 633 (Washington, D. C., 1911), 322 ff.

An effort to improve the housing environment of coke workers is described in, "Better Living Conditions for Coke Workers: Some Account of the Improved Relations between the H. C. Frick Coke Company and Its Employees Due to Welfare Measures," *Iron Age*, **95** (January 7, 1915), 48–49. The initiative was taken by Thomas Lynch, president of the company.

Miningtown.

Indeed, the least efficient business organization was better administered than the most vital public enterprise. Even the much maligned Pittsburgh Street Railway Company compiled a detailed street survey as a basis for future expansion; yet the Pittsburgh Bureau of Health did not publish one report between 1899 and 1907 "showing how people died."[36] If industry was indifferent to health, housing, and social welfare, little was accomplished. There was no alternative system of authority and decision making, no consensus on what action was needed.

The Pittsburgh Survey had stressed the discrepancy in America's greatest industrial district between economic cohesion and planning, on the one hand, and community fragmentation, on the other. It was a multidimensional fragmentation—topographical, governmental, ethnic, and class—which inhibited response to environmental and social problems. Outside the industrial sector, there was no coherent mechanism for defining issues and mobilizing resources. This book is concerned with efforts in the twentieth century to devise techniques of intervention, focusing primarily upon the physical environment and the role of both governmental and nonstatutory institutions. It is concerned, in short, with what the Pittsburgh experience reveals about the process of environmental change in the twentieth century urban community, with specific reference to government and to voluntary agencies imbued with a public purpose.

36 Kellogg, "The Social Engineer in Pittsburgh," 153 (cited in footnote 9).

TWO

The Reform Process—The Voluntary Sector

The reform process in Pittsburgh was governed by three closely related circumstances. Purposeful environmental intervention could not occur without the participation of the major business interests. They were the primary source of money, power, and expertise. The timing and nature of reform were necessarily conditioned by their aspirations. Second, the emergence of reform movements in the early twentieth century was profoundly influenced by the realization of business leaders that civic fragmentation had a dual effect. It perpetuated the authority of the business sector, which was the single comparatively cohesive force, but it also limited and frustrated that authority. Paradoxically, feeble community institutions were a source of business power and a challenge to it. Finally, businessmen and business organizations, after the turn of the century, discovered a practical relationship between economic and community affairs, one that stimulated their involvement in hitherto neglected aspects of civic life.

The reform process in such disparate areas as politics, welfare, and environmental melioration had little to do with revitalizing democracy. It was an elite rather than a mass movement and was designed to centralize rather than diffuse power. In general terms, reform was associated with ideals of bureaucratic rationalization espoused by an alliance of business and professional leaders. Even the Pittsburgh Survey, which criticized business as the source of many community pathologies, adopted the corporation as the model for the centralization, coordination, and planning that would modernize governmental and social institutions.

A study of Pittsburgh municipal reform in the early twentieth century by Samuel Hays illuminates the role of the business and professional elite. Reformers, he points out, used the rhetoric of democracy and the public interest, but "they in no sense meant that all segments of society should be involved equally in municipal decision-making. They meant that their concept of the city's welfare would be best achieved in the business community controlled city government." An examination of 745 members of two leading reform organizations—the Civic Club and Voters' League —reveals that 65 percent were listed in the upper-class city directories, which contained 2 percent of the families. The reformers belonged to a post-Civil War elite rather than the older, landed mercantile class. Fifty-two percent were corporation and financial executives or their wives; 48 percent were professional men.

These business and professional groups, Hays explains, were committed to the rationalization of institutions and decision making in modern life. An important element in their outlook was the "rapid expansion of the geographical scope of affairs which they wished to influence and manipulate." The compact pedestrian community was giving way to the metropolitan area whose complexities and "wide range of activities" were beginning to defy comprehension and control. The reformers objected particularly to a system of ward elections, taxation, and school administration that nurtured machine politics and diffused decision making. It enabled lower- and middle-class groups to assert their particularistic interests. In 1911 the reformers made significant progress in their revolt against local autonomy. Ward election of councilmen and school boards was abolished, and the tax system was revised. As a result of the changes, the city council and school board were dominated by "members of the upper class, the advanced professional men, and the larger business groups."[1]

[1] Samuel P. Hays, "The Politics of Reform in Municipal Government in the Progressive Era," Pacific Northwest Quarterly, 55 (October 1964), 160, 161, 165. Pittsburgh politics in the last two decades of the nineteenth century were dominated by Christopher L. Magee and William Flinn. Magee, a Republican politician, died in 1901. Flinn, a contractor served in the Pennsylvania legislature from 1890 to 1902. See Oliver McClintock, "Municipal Reform in Pittsburgh," Conference for Good City Government, Proceedings (1898), 257–266; Lincoln Steffens, "Pittsburgh: A City Ashamed," in Steffens, The Shame of the Cities (New York: Sagamore Press, 1957), orig. pub., 1904, 101–133; Eugene C. Thrasher, "The Magee-

Thus the reform process, initiated in the early twentieth century, was dominated by a business and professional elite. Confronted by localism and fragmentation of authority, it aspired to a bureaucratic rationalization of civic functions. This implied new institutions and arrangements that centralized decision making and made possible the application of professional expertise to community problems. Such rationalization was designed not only to extend the influence and protect the interests of the business and professional leadership, but to comply with their quest for order and system on the metropolitan scale.

Aspirations for bureaucratic rationalization were compromised, however, by a contradictory element of the business creed that idealized entrepreneurial autonomy and favored private rather than public decision making. An effort to reconcile these two opposing ideologies was made through a differential allocation of functions to public and voluntary institutions. Bureaucratic rationalization could not be achieved without enhancing governmental authority, but it would be limited to a comparatively negative, regulatory function. Voluntary institutions, on the other hand, would play a more positive, constructive role. More than government, citywide civic agencies would coordinate activities and centralize decision making over a wide range of civic affairs. The crucial consideration is that voluntary intervention seemed most compatible both with aspirations for bureaucratic rationalization and with the commitment to private interest group pre-

Flinn Political Machine, 1895–1903," unpublished M.A., University of Pittsburgh, 1951.

Following Magee's death, the Voters' League under A. Leo Weil led a reform campaign that installed William A. Guthrie as mayor in 1906. Clinton Rogers Woodruff, "Guthrie of Pittsburgh," *The World To-Day,* 17 (November 1909), 1171–73; Charles Edward Russell, "What Are You Going to Do About It? 2. Graft as an Expert Trade in Pittsburgh," *Cosmopolitan Magazine,* 49 (August 1910), 283–292.

The restoration of the Republican party to power in 1909 under Mayor William Magee was followed by the institution of charges of malfeasance and mismanagement brought by the Voters' League in 1912 against the heads of the Department of Public Works, Department of Public Safety, and Department of Health. "Civic Grit and Pittsburgh Churches," *Survey,* 28 (June 22, 1912), 463–465; "What 'Wide Open' Meant in Pittsburgh," *Survey,* 28 (August 24, 1912), 653–654; "The Trail of the Pittsburgh Directors," *Survey,* 29 (November 9, 1912), 169–70.

rogatives. The reform process led to an increase in governmental welfare and service functions, but they were circumscribed and negative in character.

This effort to reconcile the conflicting elements of the business-professional creed through a differential allocation of functions to the public and voluntary sectors proved largely ineffectual. One important constraint was the division within the business community between the large metropolitan and nationally oriented corporate enterprise, and the small entrepreneur and tradesman. The interests of the "cosmopolitans" and "locals" did not always coincide.[2] Rationalization of the housing market, for example, posed a threat to the small speculative developer. The result for many decades was stalemate or, at best, incremental change. Only the crisis situation that materialized after World War II, and produced major realignments in the historic role and relationship of the public and voluntary sectors, made decisive environmental intervention possible.

In early twentieth century Pittsburgh, three city-wide organizations embodied the reform aspirations of the business and professional leadership. They were the Civic Club, Civic Commission, and Chamber of Commerce. The latter provides an especially revealing example of a reform process inspired by larger industrial and commercial interests with a metropolitan and national orientation. The Chamber's campaigns for a Greater Pittsburgh and an Associated Charities illustrate the quest for

[2] On the significance of the division between cosmopolitans and locals in community life, see Robert K. Merton, "Patterns of Influence: Local and Cosmopolitan Influentials," in Merton, *Social Theory and Social Structure* (Glencoe, Illinois; Free Press, 1957), 387–420. The related bifurcation between the business-civic and political sectors, an American urban phenomenon, is discussed in David L. Westby, "The Civic Sphere in the American City," *Social Forces,* 45 (December 1966), 161–169; and Peter H. Rossi, "Power and Politics: A Road to Social Reform," *Social Service Review,* 35 (December 1961), 359–369. Rossi points out that "as the industrial and professional elite withdrew from local politics as political office holders, the private sector developed as the sphere over which they could exercise control." The political leader, furthermore, tended to be a local, whose mobility was based upon acquaintance and occupation in the community; the elite of the private sector, on the other hand, tended to be cosmopolitans whose mobility and status were tied to "organizational networks which transcend local boundaries" (p. 363, 364).

bureaucratic rationalization. Its campaign for housing betterment through regulatory legislation and sponsorship of voluntary model housing companies illustrates the differential allocation of functions to public and private institutions. The Chamber desired centralization and coordination of decision making in civic affairs, but they would have to come largely through the influence of noncoercive voluntary agencies.

The Pittsburgh Survey acknowledged that "by its bold pioneering in various directions . . . the Pittsburgh Chamber of Commerce, notably in 1907–08 under the presidency of H. D. W. English, came to offer a new leadership to Pittsburgh."[3] A prominent insurance executive, English personified the businessman-reformer who shared, with the professional, a dedication to centralization and the application of expertise in the conduct of civic affairs. As president of the Civic Commission, Chamber of Commerce, and Kingsley House settlement, and local sponsor of the Pittsburgh Survey, English as much as any single individual cemented the link between the business-professional elite and civic reform in Pittsburgh. He was responsible, as president of the Chamber, for the appointment of a Flood Commission in 1908, praised by the Survey as "illustrative of the statesmanlike undertakings which the Chamber has promoted."[4] Flood control was, of course, a regional undertaking, and one that required the collaboration of "business and professional men."[5] As in the case of other community problems, effective intervention was incompatible with the persistence of localized, diffused decision making, particularly by amateurs.

While English played a leading role in the conversion of the Chamber of Commerce into a civic reform organization, the Chamber and other business-civic groups were merging in order to increase their effectiveness. Indeed, the Pittsburgh Survey interpreted the "co-ordination of various commercial and civic bodies" as the "most significant evidence of the passing of the old individualism and sectionalism." In 1907 the Chamber ab-

[3] Robert A. Woods, "Pittsburgh: An Interpretation of Its Growth," in *The Pittsburgh District: Civic Frontage* (New York: Russell Sage Foundation, Survey Associates, 1914), 27.
[4] *Ibid.*
[5] Chamber of Commerce of Pittsburgh, *Annual Report, May, 1909*, 35.

sorbed its rival, the Merchants' and Manufacturers' Association. The next year, fifteen local boards of trade formed an Allied Boards of Trade "in order to pool issues, believing that each locality could best be served when the whole city is served."[6] The Chamber and Allied Boards of Trade were linked to the Civic Club, Civic Commission, and other groups through interlocking membership or joint committees.

The Chamber of Commerce sought to broaden this thrust toward unification and coordination in the civic affairs of the community. No area was more desperately in need of administrative rationalization than the charities of Pittsburgh. The problem was an excess of neighborhood autonomy and democracy; any individual, group, or church was free to participate in the system of charitable free enterprise. Social workers shared with businessmen a conviction that efficient, scientific philanthropy required a greater degree of centralization and authority for trained professionals.

The Civic Club had labored futilely since 1898 to "systematize the administration of Pittsburgh charities."[7] A charity organization society or associated charities was bitterly resisted by older relief agencies, notably the Pittsburgh Association for the Improvement of the Poor. This was the kind of agency condemned by the Survey as the "unregenerate charitable institution." It represented an older tradition of paternalism, parochialism, and amateurism out of touch with any "modernizing movements."[8] Resistance was finally overcome in 1907, when an Associated Charities was formed.[9] No longer isolated, the Civic Club had

---

[6] Allen T. Burns, "Coalition of Pittsburgh's Civic Forces," in *Pittsburgh District: Civic Frontage,* 54.

[7] Civic Club of Allegheny County, *Fifteen Years of Civic History, October 1895–December 1910,* 23.

[8] Edward T. Devine, "Results of the Pittsburgh Survey," *American Journal of Sociology,* 14 (March 1909), 662; *As Others See Us: An Anniversary Review of Some of the Positive Achievements of the Associated Charities of Pittsburgh during Four Pioneer Years of Service* (1912), 68.

[9] The Associated Charities evolved out of mass meetings held on June 20, 1907 and October 18, 1907. At the latter, a Committee of Fifteen was established to develop a plan of organization. Francis McLean of New York, identified with the movement for federations or councils of social agencies in the early twentieth century, played an important role as consultant. The

been supported by the Chamber of Commerce and, generally, the "business community, the heavy contributors to charity." The Associated Charities stood for "business economy, efficiency and constructive philanthropy." It employed progressive techniques of investigation, coordination, and personal service to lead the poor "back to the ranks of the self-sustaining." A member of the Chamber of Commerce compared the Associated Charities to Dun and Bradstreet; the intelligent businessman used both organizations to secure "efficiency in the expenditure of money."[10]

After the Associated Charities was established, the Chamber of Commerce exerted pressure on welfare organizations to cooperate with the new agency. In 1909 it appointed a special committee on charities whose chairman, Oliver McClintock (president of the Civic Club), described the Associated Charities as a "business necessity" that made possible a "common interest and a coordinated work."[11] The Chamber, in 1910, appointed a regular Committee on Charities Endorsement and Advice. Its objective was the rationalization and professionalization of a field that was so often a "free-for-all, the entrance to which is easy, resulting in many people, lacking ability, experience, equipment or training, attempting to carry on a work for which they are not adapted." Committee endorsement required that a charitable agency fill a recognized need, adopt efficient accounting procedures, and cooperate "in promoting efficiency and economy of administration in the charities of the city as a whole."[12]

An Associated Charities, it was hoped, would lead to rationalization of one major civic function on a city-wide basis. The

---

Associated Charities was formally organized in December, 1907 and incorporated early in 1908. Civic Club, *Fifteen Years of Civic History,* 24–26; Francis H. McLean, "The Charities of Pittsburgh," *Charities and the Commons,* 21 (February 6, 1909), 858–869.

Further centralization occurred in 1909 when a Children's Bureau was organized through the initiative of the Associated Charities. "Associated Charities Advances in Pittsburgh," *Survey,* 22 (June 26, 1909), 446–447.

[10] McLean, "Charities of Pittsburgh," 867; *As Others See Us,* 31, 45, 41.
[11] *Ibid.,* 44, 45.
[12] Pittsburgh Chamber of Commerce, *Report of Committee on Charities Endorsement and Advice on Charities Situation in Pittsburgh and Vicinity* (1911), n.p.

campaign of the Chamber of Commerce for a Greater Pittsburgh represented an effort to centralize decision making over a much wider area and range of activities. Once again, reform was contingent upon the suppression of local autonomy and democratic self-determination. The Chamber justified a Greater Pittsburgh, coterminous with the whole of Allegheny County, in terms of civic pride and, ultimately, business growth. It was a source of annoyance to the city booster that Pittsburgh was "dwarfed and made small in comparison with other cities, where outlying but dependent suburbs have been merged in one municipal organization." The corporate limits of Pittsburgh contained only 300,000 persons, while a county homogeneous in its "business activities" claimed 800,000. A Greater Pittsburgh of that size would "rank as the fourth in population and third in manufactures in the United States." The consolidation of the "entire county into a great city" would stimulate investment and industrial development.[13]

As early as 1894 the Chamber appointed a committee to promote a Greater Pittsburgh, and urged its consideration by the select councils of Pittsburgh and Allegheny. It introduced annexation bills into the state legislature in 1903 and again in 1905, when enabling legislation was passed for the annexation of Allegheny. After this was construed as unconstitutional by the Pennsylvania Supreme Court, the Chamber's Committee on Municipal Affairs prepared another annexation bill for the special session of the legislature in 1906. The measure needed and acquired a simple majority of the combined vote of the two cities in the election of June, 1906 (an arrangement that residents of Allegheny had vehemently protested).[14] The forced annexation of Allegheny roused the fears of suburban officials and citizens,

---

[13] Pittsburgh Chamber of Commerce, *Year Book and Directory, 1901*, 24, 25.

[14] Pittsburgh Chamber of Commerce, *Fifty Years of the Chamber of Commerce of Pittsburgh, 1874–1924* (Pittsburgh, 1924), 67, 68; *What Has the Chamber of Commerce Done?*, n.p., n.d.; Pittsburgh Chamber of Commerce, *Year Book and Directory, 1903*, 25; Pittsburgh Chamber of Commerce, *Year Book and Directory, 1905*, 23, 30; *A Year's Record of Usefulness. Annual Report of the President to the Pittsburgh Chamber of Commerce, May, 1907*, 6–7.

who organized a league of suburban communities for self-protection and stymied later efforts to create a Greater Pittsburgh.

If centralization could not be achieved politically, then voluntary agencies might be used to cope with problems affecting the entire metropolitan area. The Chamber, for example, appointed a Pittsburgh Industrial Development Commission in 1911. It consisted of 12 businessmen, whose major responsibility was to attract industry to the Pittsburgh district through an aggressive, centrally directed "campaign of publicity."[15]

The Pittsburgh experience suggests that voluntary institutions performed two pivotal tasks in the business-dominated reform tradition. Voluntary agencies like the Chamber of Commerce or Civic Club often defined the issues and areas of intervention. They set in motion the organized forces of change, including the adoption of new service and welfare functions by government. Second, voluntary action helped resolve a conflict in the ideology of the businessman-reformer. Through voluntarism, he could work toward bureaucratic rationalization or a centralization of decision making that extended his influence throughout the civic realm. At the same time, the use of noncoercive voluntary institutions to direct change was compatible with that component of the business creed that viewed private entrepreneurship as the source of economic progress and political liberty. The development of the housing and tax reform movements in Pittsburgh clarifies these points.

Three city-wide organizations and one social settlement were closely identified with housing betterment efforts in the early twentieth century—the Civic Club, Chamber of Commerce, Civic Commission, and Kingsley House. The introduction of housing as an issue of community concern was the result of voluntary, not governmental initiative; it was closely related to the aspiration of business and professional men to exert greater control over the total community environment. The strategy of housing reform limited government to the enactment of regulatory legislation, and to tax reforms that would enable the market mechanisms to operate more efficiently. Noncoercive voluntary institutions were

[15] Pittsburgh Industrial Development Commission, *First Annual Report, December 1, 1912*, 3.

delegated the more constructive responsibility of developing model housing programs that would expand the supply of good, low-cost housing.

The Civic Club was the first agency to deal with housing as a reform issue. Its initiative was largely attributable to Mrs. Franklin P. (Lucy Dorsey) Iams, wife of a Pittsburgh lawyer. Mrs. Iams became chairman of the Club's Social Science Department and Tenement Committee in 1902 (she also served as chairman of its Legislative Committee and as first vice-president). She was instrumental in the enactment of the state housing law of 1903, and in winning an appropriation from the Pittsburgh councils for inspectors.[16] The Chamber of Commerce became active in housing during the presidency of H. D. W. English in 1907–1908. Through committees on housing and municipal sanitation, the Chamber, like the Civic Club, publicized the issue and campaigned for regulatory legislation.[17] The Chamber joined with the Civic Club and other organizations in 1910 to form a Pittsburgh Housing Conference. It was designed to coordinate the housing legislation efforts of the member agencies.[18]

No voluntary institution was more active than Kingsley House in goading, rousing, and educating public opinion on housing. Established in 1893 by Rev. George Hodges, the settlement became immersed in housing reform during the years that William H. Matthews served as headworker (1902–1911).[19] Located orig-

[16] Civic Club, *Fifteen Years of Civic History*, 12, 52–53 (cited in footnote 7).

[17] *A Year's Record of Usefulness. Annual Report of the President to the Pittsburgh Chamber of Commerce, May, 1907*, 11, 17.

[18] Emily Wayland Dinwiddie and F. Elisabeth Crowell, "The Housing of Pittsburgh's Workers: Discussed from the Standpoint of Sanitary Regulation and Control," in *Pittsburgh District: Civic Frontage*, 119; Civic Club of Allegheny County, *Annual Report, 1911–1912*, 30. Represented in the Housing Conference were the Chamber of Commerce, Civic Club, Civic Commission, Kingsley House, Pittsburgh Board of Trade, Council of Jewish Women, and Associated Charities. Mrs. Iams served as vice-chairman.

[19] Matthews, a graduate of Williams College and Union Theological Seminary, had been assistant head worker at Union Settlement in New York City. The intellectual and personal influence of Robert A. Woods of Boston had been instrumental in Hodge's establishment of Kingsley House. He was encouraged and assisted by H.D.W. English. "A Letter from Dr. George Hodges, the Founder of Kingsley House, Pittsburgh," in William H.

inally at Penn Avenue and 17th Street, it moved in 1901 to the corner of Bedford Avenue and Fulton Street in the heart of Pittsburgh's immigrant Hill District. "From the first," Matthews explained, "I had been conscious of the unsanitary evil conditions within and without the alley tenements a stone's throw from Kingsley House."[20] Like other settlement workers, he saw a "vital relation" between housing and the objectives of his agency. "In any attempt to relieve the stress of poverty, the evils of intemperance, sickness, inability and incapacity to work, the settlement worker finds himself driven back to the home, the home with its dark, disease producing rooms, its unsanitary closets, its inadequate water supply, its damp, life-sapping cellar dwelling rooms. These constitute a poverty of environment productive of people without strength, people destined to physical misery, moral impoverishment and economic disability. . . ."[21]

Beginning in 1903, Kingsley House published photographs and descriptions of housing conditions. Matthews complained of the cow stable on Webster Avenue (7th Ward Dairy) and asked why the city permitted this in the midst of crowded tenement districts. He condemned the many filthy rag shops in the Hill District, located in sheds and dwellings near the tenements. Between Roberts and Arthur Streets were "rear yards and rear closets . . . in revolting condition." The bank above Grant Boulevard between 16th and 18th Streets contained numerous dry vault closets; it was a "receiving station for sewage of the filthiest kind, for garbage that is never collected and for rubbish of every description." There were hundreds of basement rooms in Pittsburgh—"dark, damp, dreary places" where families ate, slept, and worked. Close to Kingsley House were many examples of the court housing found throughout the Pittsburgh region. A single hydrant served as the water supply for dozens of families; wooden planks that covered the court loosened and became "saturated with filth." The only thing that infuriated Matthews

Matthews, *The Meaning of the Social Settlement Movement: Together with a Chronological Sketch of the Work of Kingsley House, Pittsburgh, Pa.* (Pittsburgh: Kingsley House, 1909), 33–34.
[20] William H. Matthews, *Adventures in Giving* (New York: Dodd, Mead, 1939), 65.
[21] Matthews, *The Meaning of the Social Settlement Movement,* 44.

more than the absence of legislation to deal with such conditions was the city's failure to enforce existing legislation. Too often, the Bureau of Health "neither sees these things nor pays any attention to the complaints of those who do."[22]

One might ask why businessmen supported the drive for remedial housing legislation. Why was housing included in the broader quest for bureaucratic rationalization of civic functions? The answer lies partly in the evolution of a new perspective on the relationship between business and community life. The business and professional elite associated with key voluntary agencies perceived that the economic future of Pittsburgh was linked to housing and other hitherto ignored environmental factors. We must realize, H. D. W. English informed the members of the Chamber of Commerce, that a "commercial supremacy is impossible in a community that lacks civic spirit or is indifferent to civic decay." Housing and public health were business propositions. Each death from typhoid, for example, had a "deterrent influence upon the sales of every merchant in Pittsburgh." Manufacturers refused to locate in Pittsburgh "because of our housing conditions." Substandard housing, faulty water and sewerage facilities, and air pollution were all a "species of indirect taxation upon business interests, not only as tax-payers, but in their effect upon output."[23] Physicians, sanitarians, and social workers agreed that the influence of the worker's home environment extended to the factory, reducing the efficiency of the labor force.

The truth was that the machinery of housing production in Greater Pittsburgh had "completely broken down," a matter that vitally affected the "business interests of every large concern in this City." The problem was especially acute in the case of unskilled immigrant workers. They resided, often, in coverted one-family dwellings, five to twelve men in a single room. In their neighborhoods, "toilet facilities, water, ventilation, are most often inadequate; here typhoid, tuberculosis and other diseases are

---

22 William H. Matthews, A Pamphlet Illustrative of Housing Conditions in Neighborhoods Popularly Known as the Tenement House Districts of Pittsburgh, February, 1907, 6, 8, 10, 12, 18; Kingsley House Record, 7 (January 1903), 1; Kingsley House Record, 8 (March 1905), 1.

23 A Year's Record of Great Achievements. Annual Report of the President to the Chamber of Commerce of Pittsburgh, May, 1908, 4, 19.

most common; here the municipal authorities find it most difficult
to build up health standards, as there is apparently no place else
for these men to live; and here the conditions are such as to be
absolutely inimical to the delevopment (sic) and health of such
children as live in these districts."[24]

The housing legislation favored by the Chamber and other
civic organizations might prevent the worst conditions, but could
do nothing to increase the supply of good, low-cost housing. The
businessman-reformer recognized this fact, but did not conclude
that government had any responsibility to increase the housing
supply except indirectly through tax policy. The constructive
role in this vital area was delegated to voluntary agencies. Bureaucratic rationalization would be achieved—decision making
centralized and the housing environment controlled—if large-
scale, nonspeculative developers could be induced to absorb a
larger portion of the housing market. Model housing under
noncoercive voluntary sponsorship was thus the key to housing
betterment. Unfortunately, neither in Pittsburgh nor in other
American communities did model housing efforts ever command
sufficient capital to influence the housing market, which remained
dominated by small-scale, speculative developers.[25] The advocacy of model housing helped reconcile the two conflicting elements of the business creed—rationalization and entrepreneurial
autonomy—but did not accomplish much more.

The Civic Club brought Jacob Riis to Pittsburgh in 1900 with
the intention of organizing a model tenement company.[26] This
produced no response, but a Pittsburgh Tenement Improvement
Company was launched in 1903. Its sole achievement was the
erection of a five-story brick structure at Logan and Franklin
Streets. The Franklin Flats were supposed to prove that "good
housing could be made a successful investment"; but the Company encountered difficulty in paying dividends and meeting its

---

[24] *Ibid.*, 20, 21.
[25] The model housing movement is discussed in Roy Lubove, *The Progressives and the Slums: Tenement House Reform in New York, 1890–1917*
(Pittsburgh: University of Pittsburgh Press, 1962).
[26] Civic Club, *Fifteen Years of Civic History*, 36–37; Civic Club of Allegheny County, Minutes, April 6, 1900.

financial obligations.[27] A second minor model housing experiment was the five-story Phipps Apartment on the North Side. Built in 1908 by steel magnate Henry Phipps, this 60-apartment tenement was sold in 1937 by the Phipps Land Trust.[28]

The Pittsburgh Survey did not find the prospects for extensive model housing promising. The president of a major steel company expressed his firm's reluctance to enter the housing business except in areas where it was imperative in order "to attract and hold labor." A prominent realtor was quoted as saying that "there certainly are other more attractive investments for private capital than the building of small houses."[29] The Chamber of Commerce and other civic agencies nonetheless persisted in their campaign for model low-cost housing. The need was urgent and there was no alternative method for increasing the supply except through government. Such an expedient was incompatible with the entrepreneurial component of business ideology, and it would have created a serious conflict within the business community between exponents of rationalization and the small developers who dominated the housing market.

The Chamber of Commerce's Committee on Housing reported in 1911 that emphasis would shift from regulatory legislation to "more constructive work—that is, the building of new sanitary dwellings for workmen." Produce enough good new housing and the "fewer hospitals, insane asylums and jails, for from bad environment and housing are such institutions fed."[30] In 1914 the Chamber appointed a special commission to cooperate with the

[27] Kingsley House Record, 7 (February 1903), 2; Kingsley House Record, 8 (March 1904), 4; Kingsley House Record, 12 (February 1909), 4; Construction, 1 (April 1, 1905), 12. A Tenement Improvement Company had been organized in Pittsburgh in 1893. It apparently faded into oblivion with no record of accomplishment. Dinwiddie and Crowell, "The Housing of Pittsburgh's Workers," 90, 91 (cited in footnote 18).

[28] Bulletin Index, 111 (December 30, 1937), 8. The tenement was located at Shore Avenue, Scotland and Reedsdale Streets.

[29] Dinwiddie and Crowell, "The Housing of Pittsburgh's Workers, 121 (cited in footnote 18).

[30] Chamber of Commerce of Pittsburgh, Report of Committee on Housing Conditions on Workman's Dwellings (Approved by Chamber of Commerce, November 8, 1911), n.p.

Committee on Housing in the formation of a model housing company. Nothing came of the commission's recommendation in 1915 for a Sanitary Dwellings Company.[31]

The model housing efforts of the Pittsburgh Civic Commission proved equally futile. Appointed by Mayor Guthrie in 1909, the Commission was an outstanding example of business-professional collaboration in the reform process. It had been conceived by Robert A. Woods, the prominent Boston settlement worker, while in Pittsburgh on behalf of the Survey.[32] The Commission's president was H. D. W. English; its secretary was Allen T. Burns, a professional social worker imported from Chicago, where he had been associate director of the School of Civics and Philanthropy. Other leading businessmen and professionals served on the Commission's 14 committees.[33] During its brief existence, the Civic Commission acted as a kind of focal point for reform. As an effort to provide leverage for change by concentrating community prestige, power, and expertise, it foreshadowed the Allegheny Conference on Community Development. Both in the early twentieth century and after World War II, reform in Pittsburgh was singularly dependent upon the initiative of a limited business and professional elite.

[31] Chamber of Commerce of Pittsburgh, *Annual Report for 1913–1914*, 43; Chamber of Commerce of Pittsburgh, *Annual Report, 1914–1915*, 20, 31. The Chamber had appropriated $1000 to the Commission for the preparation of plans and surveys. The Sanitary Dwellings Company was supposed to be modeled after the Washington Sanitary Improvement Company.

[32] Paul Kellogg, "Shapers of Things," *Survey Graphic*, 27 (January 1938), 17.

[33] The Committees included Rapid Transit; Charitable Institutions; City Planning; Education; Legislation; Municipal Art and Design; City and District Housing; District Improvements; Industrial Accidents and Overstrain; Lower Courts of Justice; Municipal Publication; Public Hygiene and Sanitation; Municipal Research and Efficiency; and Ward Organization.

Each committee was headed by a member of the Commission. Officers and members were H. D. W. English, president; D. P. Black, 1st vice-president; John W. Beatty, 2nd vice-president; H. J. Heinz, 3rd vice-president; J. J. Donnell, treasurer; Allen T. Burns, general secretary; O. H. Allerton; T. E. Ballquist; William L. Jones; A. J. Kelly, Jr.; J. W. Kinnear; Morris Knowles; H. L. Kreusler; Joseph W. Marsh; Marcus Rauh; Lee S. Smith; George R. Wallace; Charles F. Weller. See Pittsburgh Civic Commission, *Plan and Scope* (n.p., n.d.).

The sweeping mandate of the Civic Commission was to "plan and promote improvements in civic and industrial conditions which affect the health, convenience, education and general welfare of the Pittsburgh industrial district; to create public opinion in favor of such improvements; and thus to establish such living and working conditions as may set a standard for other American industrial centers."[34] In large measure the mandate was interpreted in terms of environmental intervention and change—housing, tax reforms that influenced the housing market, and city planning. Like the Chamber of Commerce, the Civic Commission devoted considerable attention to model housing. The possibilities of using Pittsburgh's steep slopes for workers' homes particularly intrigued its Housing Committee, and local newspapers in December, 1911 featured the Committee's plans for hillside dwellings.[35] Between the Chamber of Commerce and the Civic Commission no housing was produced, with one possible exception—F. R. Babcock, a president of the Chamber of Commerce, built a group of some 16 single-family homes at Breckenridge and Morgan Streets.[36]

The supply of good, low-cost housing was not perceptibly increased through the initiative of voluntary civic agencies, who anticipated that a larger segment of the housing market would come under the control of large-scale, nonspeculative companies. There was, however, another method to increase the housing supply without involving government directly in the housing business. An appropriate tax policy might reduce land costs and encourage building operations. The Civic Commission was closely identified with this strategy of incentive taxation. Tax

[34] Ibid.
[35] Pittsburgh Leader, December 17, 1911; Pittsburgh Gazette Times, December 26, 1911. Also, Pittsburgh Civic Commission, Civic Bulletin, 1 (November 1911), 1–3. The Housing Committee was composed of H. L. Kreusler, chairman; Otto F. Felix; W. D. George; R. M. Trimble; Thomas Ward. The Committee produced two house plans: "One is for a building, or row of small houses, fronting on two streets only 32 feet apart but one on a considerably higher level than the other. The other scheme is for lines of attached houses fronting on terraces, the rows running up the hill at right angles to projected streets" (Ibid., 1).
[36] "Building Houses on Pittsburgh's Hillsides," Survey, 33 (October 10, 1914), 42–43.

reform was significant in another respect. It was part of the 1911 reform package which led to abolition of the ward council and school board system. If decisions affecting the community environment were to be centralized, it would also be necessary to overhaul a tax system that generally favored local autonomy.

The Pittsburgh Survey sharply criticized the unreformed tax mechanism for its inequities and irrationalities. A survival of the preindustrial era, it divided real estate into three classifications. City property paid the full assessed rate; rural or suburban property paid two-thirds; and agricultural property was taxed at one-half the rate. Equally idiosyncratic was the subdistrict school tax in which there was no necessary relationship between a neighborhood's needs, tax rates, and ability to pay.

Shelby Harrison's detailed investigation for the Survey included three illustrations drawn from the assessor's rolls of the inequitable incidence of taxation.[37] The small home of A. Savich was situated off 48th Street, fronting unpaved, unlighted Plum Alley. Houses were crowded together in a smoke-laden atmosphere, and weeds barely penetrated the cindered backyards. District schools were mediocre. The city assessors in 1910 valued the 25' × 50' lot at $550, and the house at $400. Savich's city tax totaled $15.15, a rate of approximately $1.60 per $100 of evaluation. John Brown, millionaire, resided on North Highland Avenue. His spacious home was surrounded by acres of land, and his children enjoyed the best public schools in the city. In 1910 the assessors valued his land at $202,500, and his home at $54,400. At the two-thirds suburban rate, his total city tax was $2,688.89, or about $1.05 per $100. Finally, an absentee estate owned the 105 acres and rambling house overlooking the Allegheny River Valley. This so-called agricultural land separated two densely populated districts. The tax in 1910 totaled $2,192.71, representing 83½ cents per $100 assessed value. Harrison noted that support of the dismal school facilities in his area cost Savich $2.14 in 1910, representing a subdistrict school tax of 23 cents per $100. Brown, for much superior schools, contributed $342.53 or 13 cents per $100. The estate was taxed $393.90, or 15 cents per $100.

[37] Shelby M. Harrison, "The Disproportion of Taxation in Pittsburgh," in *Pittsburgh District: Civic Frontage*, 156–213.

Tax reform was essential to environmental change. Harrison pointed out that if the classification system did not exist in 1910, city income would have increased by $3,000,000, enough to multiply playground expenditures tenfold, add half a million dollars to the health department budget, and improve many other services. A campaign for tax reform had been launched in 1909 by the Pittsburgh Board of Trade. Its Committee on City Assessments complained that the classification system "works an injustice in many instances to the individual property owners, particularly to the small owners."[38] The Civic Commission, Chamber of Commerce (through Committees on Real Estate and Taxation), and numerous other civic groups added their support. The case for tax reform before the 1911 legislature was strengthened by Harrison's Survey report, completed the year before.[39]

After elimination of the classification system and subdistrict school tax in 1911, the Civic Commission pressed for a graded tax that would impose a heavier burden on land than improvements. Abetting the Commission was an influential nucleus of Pittsburgh Single-Taxers, who had also played a part in the 1911 reforms.[40] They were represented on the Commission's Commit-

[38] Allied Boards of Trade, Journal, 1 (March 1910), 7. The resolution of the Pittsburgh Board of Trade for uniform taxation was endorsed by the Allied Boards of Trade.

[39] Chamber of Commerce of Pittsburgh, Annual Report for 1910, 44; Harrison, "Taxation in Pittsburgh," 156. Along with the Civic Commission, Chamber of Commerce, Pittsburgh Board of Trade, and Allied Boards of Trade, the abolition of the classification system was supported by the Pittsburgh Teachers' Association, Pittsburgh Principals' Association, Schoolmasters' Club of Western Pennsylvania, Federation of Women's Clubs, and Junior Order of American Mechanics (Ibid.).

[40] Pittsburgh Single-Taxers, such as W. D. George and R. E. Smith, had stimulated interest in tax reform by importing lecturers to address the Chamber of Commerce, Boards of Trade, and other groups. Bernard B. McGuinnis, "The Movement in Pittsburgh," Single Tax Review, 12 May–June 1912), 44–46; John Z. White, "Tax Reform in Pennsylvania," The Public, 16 (February 14, 1913), 151; Percy R. Williams, "Pittsburgh's Pioneering in Scientific Taxation," I, American Journal of Economics and Sociology, 21 (January 1962), 54–55. Williams points out that most of the Pittsburgh Single-Taxers were affiliated with the Democratic Party, the local Single Tax Club and, later, the Henry George Foundation, chartered in 1926 and headquartered in Pittsburgh.

tee on Housing by Harry H. Willcock, an industrialist, and William D. George, a realtor-lawyer. These men were instrumental in coverting Mayor Magee to the graded tax. Before committing himself, however, Magee sent his leading tax adviser, T. C. McMahon, to Vancouver and other western Canadian cities to examine precedents. His report attributed the economic progress of these communities, in part, to their tax policy.[41]

A bill prepared by W. D. George and attorney Marcus W. Acheson passed the state legislature in 1913.[42] It applied to second-class cities (Pittsburgh and Scranton) and fixed the tax rate on buildings at one-half that on land. To prevent undue hardships, the reduction was spread over a 12 year period, reaching the 50 percent level in 1925. A vigorous effort was made in 1915 to abolish the graded tax. It was led by Magee's successor, Mayor Joseph G. Armstrong, banking interests, and representatives of large landed proprietors, including Frank F. Nicola, president of Schenley Farms Real Estate, and Edward F. Daume of the Commonwealth Real Estate Company, agent for the Schenley Estate. The Chamber of Commerce reversed its position and supported repeal in 1915. Former Mayor Magee and W. D. George defended the measure in Harrisburg. George's political role was crucial in 1913 and 1915. As a member of the Board of Governors of the Pittsburgh Real Estate Board, he helped acquire the endorsement of that influential organization. Although the legislature passed a repeal bill, it was vetoed by Governor Brumbaugh.[43]

The Civic Commission had maintained that the graded tax would "remove the chief obstacles to Pittsburgh's progress."[44]

[41] *Ibid.*, 55–56; White, "Tax Reform in Pennsylvania," 489–90.

[42] Williams, "Pittsburgh's Pioneering in Scientific Taxation," 55.

[43] Percy R. Williams, "Pittsburgh's Pioneering in Scientific Taxation," II, *American Journal of Economics and Sociology,* 21 (April 1962), 211–215; *Pittsburgh Dispatch,* January 17, June 11, 1915; *Pittsburgh Press,* April 27, May 18, June 10, June 11, 1915; *Pittsburgh Post,* May 21, June 11, 1915; *The Public,* 18 (April 30, 1915), 422–423, (May 7, 1915), 446, (May 28, 1915), 521.

[44] "Tax Revision to Promote Pittsburgh's Progress: A Report of the Committee on Housing Adopted by the Pittsburgh Civic Commission December 11, 1911," in Pittsburgh Civic Commission, *Civic Bulletin,* 1 (January 1912), 1.

Rents were an important component in Pittsburgh's notoriously high cost of living. They reflected inflated land values in a community whose terrain was exceptionally rugged. Since one-third of the city's land area consisted of slopes with a gradient of 25 percent or more, the relative scarcity of level land made it "all the more important to find a method for keeping land prices from interfering with development." Unless land costs were reduced, industries would hesitate to locate in Pittsburgh for fear that their skilled workers would "balk" at paying excessive rents for inferior accommodations.[45]

A second source of inflated land values, more amenable to control, was the speculative withdrawal of large tracts by a few individuals or families. Yet the future of Pittsburgh depended on whether land could be obtained at a reasonable price "rather than at a price based on speculation as to what return the land will yield in the indefinite future."[46] If land were taxed at twice the rate of buildings, the holder of vacant land would be penalized, land costs would drop, and the supply of better housing at lower costs would increase.

It is doubtful that the graded tax made much difference in the long run. Percy R. Williams, a member of the Pittsburgh Board of Assessors for many years, and secretary of the Henry George Foundation, argues that the tax was a "very real influence" in controlling land speculation and stimulating improvements. The home owner and tax payer benefited further from the appropriation of the "unearned increment" for community uses.[47] Yet housing conditions in Pittsburgh did not greatly improve in the decades following imposition of the tax; and they were not noticeably superior compared to cities without a graded tax.

Several factors minimized the impact of the experiment. For one thing, it applied only to city property, and not to the school or county taxes (which, by the 1960's, totaled one-half the combined levy on Pittsburgh real estate). Second, the Pittsburgh

[45] *Ibid.*, 3, 2.
[46] *Ibid.*, 3.
[47] Percy R. Williams, "The Graded Tax in the Redevelopment of Pittsburgh," *American Journal of Economics and Sociology*, 22 (April 1963), 260. Also, Williams, "Pittsburgh's Experience with the Graded Tax Plan," *American Journal of Economics and Sociology*, 22 (January 1963), 149–172.

terrain was probably more influential in determining land prices than monopoly; there existed an absolute shortage of level land for business and residential use. Finally, the graded tax was sabotaged by a tendency to undervalue land, which did not increase proportionately with rises in the general price level. Ironically, a sharp increase in Pittsburgh rents occurred between 1919 and 1925, just as the "burden of the tax was becoming heavier and heavier upon the holder of idle land."[48]

The model housing and graded tax strategies, which left the initiative and constructive responsibilities to private developers, failed to increase the supply of good, low-cost housing. Regulatory housing legislation, the primary governmental responsibility, was never designed to cope with the supply problem. The inability of private, voluntary institutions to perform as expected weakened the capacity of the public sector to discharge even its limited regulatory function. Substandard housing could not be effectively controlled or eradicated through regulation without a reservoir of alternative housing accommodations.

[48] Lawrence R. Guild, "The Operation of the Pittsburgh Graded Tax Plan," *Journal of Land and Public Utility Economics,* 6 (February 1930), 14. "It is strange," Guild argued, "that, in the very period when prices in general were rising most rapidly, land valuations in Pittsburgh stood still. . . . It is hard to see how the rise of the general price level, which is now stabilized at a point more than 50% above that of 1913, when added to the natural increase of land values accompanying normal city growth, can add but 20% to the value of land in that City" (p. 12).

For other evaluations of the graded tax in Pittsburgh, see Percy R. Williams, "Pittsburgh's Graded Tax in Full Operation," *National Municipal Review,* 14 (December 1925), 726–732; McAlister Coleman, "Pittsburgh Has a Plan: A New Way to Pay City Debts," *Forum,* 79 (April 1928), 594–601; Edward F. Daume, "A Critical Analysis of the Operation of the Pittsburgh Graded Tax Law," American Academy of Political and Social Science, *Annals,* 148 (March 1930), 145–156; Thomas C. McMahon, "The Operation of the Graded Tax Law in Pittsburgh," *Annals,* 148 (March 1930), 139–144.

THREE

The Reform Process—The Public Sector

Sporadic efforts in the nineteenth century to regulate housing conditions in American cities were followed, after 1900, by a more systematic campaign. Lawrence Veiller of the New York Charity Organization Society introduced a new element of technical proficiency and centralization. The New York State Tenement House Law of 1901, devised by Veiller, served as a model code for numerous communities. Veiller exerted additional influence as a consultant to citizen groups throughout the country.[1] In Pittsburgh, he assisted Mrs. Iams and the Civic Club in preparing the Pennsylvania housing law of 1903, governing second-class cities.[2]

Tenements created some of the most intractable problems of regulation, but in Pittsburgh, as elsewhere, the prevalent form of slum housing was the one- and two-family dwelling. Apart from general dilapidation, low-income housing suffered from the use of dank cellar rooms for living and working purposes, absence of light and ventilation, overcrowding, and inadequate water and plumbing facilities. Nothing frustrated reformers and public officials more than the widespread use in Pittsburgh of archaic, disease-breeding privy vaults.

To cope with cellar occupancy, the 1903 legislation required

---

[1] Veiller's role in the housing reform movement is discussed in Roy Lubove, *The Progressives and the Slums: Tenement House Reform in New York City, 1890–1917* (Pittsburgh: University of Pittsburgh Press, 1962).

[2] The Civic Club was also advised by Hector McIntosh, a member of the Octavia Hill Association of Philadelphia. The legislation was prepared by the Civic Club's Tenement Committee, including Mrs. Iams, E. Z. Smith, and S. S. Mehard. Civic Club of Allegheny County, *Fifteen Years of Civic History, October 1895–December, 1910*, 52–53.

a minimum height of 8′ 3″ for each room, the installation of
water closet in each apartment, and a window in rooms openin
to the street or court. Several provisions dealt with light an
ventilation: future dwelling rooms had to contain at least on
window; tenement stairwells and halls had to be lit and vent
lated to the satisfaction of the Bureau of Health; and new ten
ments built on interior lots had to leave at least 20 percent
the lot unoccupied. To control overcrowding, the law required
least 700 cubic feet of air in occupied rooms, or a minimum
400 cubic feet for each adult, 200 for each child up to 12 yea
of age. Provisions for water and plumbing required future ten
ments to connect with city water mains where possible, and
provide an independent water supply and water closet for ea
apartment; existing tenements had to provide at least one sin
on each floor and one water closet for every two apartment
Authority to prevent the privy vaults existed before 1903;
Bureau of Health regulation in 1895 prohibited their constructio
where a sewer was adjacent, and an ordinance of 1901 mad
their continued existence unlawful. This legislation, howeve
was rarely enforced before 1906. The Department of Health di
not acquire power to vacate unfit dwellings until 1911.[3]

At best, restrictive housing legislation was a compromise b
tween the desirable and the feasible. Its usefulness was furthe
limited by difficulties of enforcement. In 1903 health affairs i
Pittsburgh were administered by a bureau in the Department
Public Safety. Enforcement of housing regulations was divide
between the Bureau of Health's Division of Sanitary Inspectio
and Division of Tenement House Inspection. Upon the establish
ment of an independent Department of Health in 1909, respons
bility was assumed by its Bureau of Sanitation operating throug
Divisions of Sanitary Inspection, Tenement House Inspectio
and Plumbing and House Drainage.[4]

[3] For the provisions of the 1903 legislation, as amended, see City of Pitt
burgh, Department of Public Health, Sanitary Code Issued to the Publ
September 1st, 1913; and Emily Wayland Dinwiddie and F. Elisabet
Crowell, "The Housing of Pittsburgh's Workers, Discussed from the Stan
point of Sanitary Regulation and Control," in The Pittsburgh District: Civ
Frontage (New York: Survey Associates, Russell Sage Foundation, 1914
87–123.
[4] In 1914, the Divisions of Tenement House Inspection and Sanitary Inspe

Enforcement was hampered by a shortage of inspectors. The 1903 housing legislation was virtually nullified during the first few years by lack of an inspection staff. Following its passage, the Civic Club had secured the appointment of two inspectors each for Pittsburgh and Allegheny. The Pittsburgh staff numbered only four by 1906. Inspired by the Pittsburgh Survey and William Matthews of Kingsley House, the Chamber of Commerce was instrumental in increasing the inspectors to thirteen by the winter of 1907–1908.[5]

More serious perhaps, in the eyes of civic reformers, was inefficient if not corrupt leadership in the Department of Health. Upon its creation in 1909, Pittsburgh medical men and others favored the appointment of Dr. James F. Edwards as director. Edwards had been superintendent of the old Bureau of Health, and he had served as chairman of the Pittsburgh Typhoid Fever Commission, appointed by Mayor Guthrie in 1908. Although Edwards was retained as head of the Bureau of Infectious Diseases, Mayor Magee chose E. R. Walters as director. As a result, according to Samuel Hopkins Adams, Pittsburgh "took a step backward toward the twilight zone of practical politics." Walters, a physician-politician, had been president of the "notorious grafting Councils, many of whose members are now under indictments or in jail." The Voters' League sought to remove Walters in 1912, charging that "sanitary conditions of the poorer districts were unbearable, that there had been few if any prosecutions under the health laws, that as many as twenty-nine violations against certain properties had been held in abeyance." The city council did not investigate the charges, and Walters remained in his post until 1914, when Edwards succeeded him. Unfortunately, the latter inherited "an inspection staff headed and loaded up with political appointees."[6]

tion were combined into a single Division of Housing and Sanitary Inspection. Previously, one group of inspectors covered tenements, and another group one- and two-family houses.

[5] Civic Club, *Fifteen Years of Civic History*, 53–55; Civic Club of Allegheny County, Minutes, December 26, 1903; *A Year's Record of Great Achievements. Annual Report of the President to the Chamber of Commerce of Pittsburgh, May, 1908*, 18; Dinwiddie and Crowell, "The Housing of Pittsburgh's Workers," 115. The original request of the Civic Club in 1903 had been for 10 or 12 inspectors.

[6] Samuel Hopkins Adams, "Tomfoolery with Public Health," *Survey*, 25

In the final analysis, it was not personnel or political problems that most seriously obstructed the enforcement of housing regulations. No American city succeeded in raising mass housing standards through regulatory legislation. The technique was inherently faulty as a strategy of housing betterment. Housing codes could not increase the supply of dwellings. High standards of legislation, effectively enforced, could only raise costs and reduce the net supply of low-income housing by discouraging builders or destruction of substandard dwellings. The crucial variable was the supply of good, low-cost housing, a surplus of which rarely existed. Without substantial vacancy rates, housing code enforcement beyond control of the worst excesses was impractical.

The experience of the Division of Tenement House Inspection suggests that the dilemma was resolved by depending largely upon education or persuasion, and trusting to Providence rather than the courts. Pittsburgh's first tenement census, taken in 1908, tabulated 45,899 persons in 3364 tenements; the equivalent figures for 1912 were approximately 60,000 persons and 4311 tenements. The majority of tenements in 1912 were constructed of brick (2731), followed by wood (1574). Of the 4311 tenements, 1197 were old-law (pre-1903), 2215 were old dwellings converted to tenements, and 899 had been built in compliance with the 1903 legislation.[7] Some of the most serious problems existed in the dwellings converted to tenements—the largest single category. These predominated in mill districts and areas in transition to commercial or industrial use.[8]

The chief tenement inspector posed the crucial issue in en-

(December 17, 1910), 453; Dinwiddie and Crowell, "The Housing of Pittsburgh's Workers," 119; "Civic Grit and the Pittsburgh Churches," Survey, 28 (June 22, 1912), 463–64.

[7] City of Pittsburgh, Department of Health, Annual Report of the Bureau of Sanitation, 1912, in City of Pittsburgh, Annual Report of the Executive Departments, Year Ending January 31, 1913, 1128, 1129.

[8] City of Pittsburgh, Department of Public Safety, Annual Report of the Bureau of Health for the Year 1907, 183–184. The greatest congestion existed in the first 12 wards and the river wards of the South Side. The latter suffered from widespread use of the "boarding house" system in which the boarding house boss rented a house or floor, filled the rooms with beds, and rented them to as many boarders as possible.

"Yellow Row," razed during construction of the Boulevard of the Allies.

forcement. "The question—where are the poorer classes to go when overcrowding in existing houses is corrected, or when dilapidated and unsanitary houses now occupied are vacated or torn down, if other houses are not available?—must be answered." No answer was forthcoming, and it became the policy "to try by persuasion, education and other mild means to get the unsanitary conditions corrected." Every effort was made to avoid litigation; "leniency was extended in every case where conditions did not immediately threaten the health of the occupants." Similarly, in answer to Pittsburgh Survey charges that the campaign against privy vaults launched in 1906–1907 had petered out, Walters explained that "we had hundreds of urgent requests for extensions of time from people who were financially unable to make these improvements." In effect, the Department of Health confronted a situation in which enforcement of the law would create as many problems as it solved, and in which the expedient of voluntary compliance proved largely ineffectual. The Division of Tenement Inspection found that its orders were ignored by "day laborer" no less than "millionaire." There was no real alternative to "sanitary education," yet its failure was "becoming daily more apparent."[9]

Smoke control, like housing legislation, represented a compromise between the desirable and feasible; and was further limited by difficulties of enforcement. Once again, the quest for bureaucratic rationalization led to the assumption of new regulatory powers by government, but the same reluctance to compromise seriously the autonomy of private business interests determined the character of public intervention. Enforcement would be achieved, if at all, by persuasion rather than coercion.

An address by Andrew Carnegie in 1899 led the Chamber of Commerce to appoint a Committee on Smoke Abatement.[10] Con-

[9] *Ibid.*, 188; City of Pittsburgh, Department of Public Health, *Annual Report, 1913,* in *Annual Reports of Departments and Offices of the City of Pittsburgh, 1913,* 248, 251; City of Pittsburgh, Department of Public Health, *Annual Report, 1912,* in City of Pittsburgh, *Annual Report of the Executive Departments, Year Ending January 31, 1913,* 1123, 1127; City of Pittsburgh, Department of Public Health, *Annual Report, 1910,* 7. Also, City of Pittsburgh, *Report on a Survey of the Department of Public Health. Prepared for the City Council by the New York Bureau of Municipal Research, June–July, 1913,* 34.

[10] "What the Chamber of Commerce has Achieved," *Pittsburgh First,* 6 (December 6, 1924), 35. Sporadic efforts had been made in the nineteenth century to deal with the smoke problem. As early as 1804, General Presley Neville had complained to the president of the Council of "the general dissatisfaction which prevails and the frequent complaints which are exhibited, in consequence of the Coal Smoke from many buildings in the Borough, particularly from the Smithies and Blacksmith Shops. . . ." Around 1869, an ordinance, never enforced, prohibited the use of bituminous coal or wood in locomotives. The situation improved somewhat from the mid-1880's to the early 1890's, when natural gas temporarily superseded coal as fuel. Having seen the light, so to speak, the Woman's Health Protective Association (which merged with the Civic Club in 1895) and the Engineers' Society of Western Pennsylvania addressed themselves to the smoke problem. A Committee on Smoke Prevention was appointed by the Engineers' Society in 1892, and in the same year the city council passed an ordinance that prohibited any smokestack connected to a stationary boiler to permit discharges from bituminous coal in the district bounded by Miltenberger, Dinwiddie, Devilliers, and 33rd Streets (but iron works were exempted from the legislation!). Enforcement, oddly enough, was placed in the hands of the Superintendent of the Bureau of Water Supply in the Department of Public Works. Another ordinance in 1895 prohibited the emission of more

sisting of engineers and manufacturers, it drafted an ordinance in 1906 that prohibited the emission of dense smoke for more than 8 minutes an hour. To help arouse an indifferent city council, the Chamber secured legislative hearings at which businessmen and civic groups testified on behalf of the measure.[11] Smoke control, like better health or housing, was a business proposition. It was part of the businessman-reformer's quest for influence over those aspects of the civic environment that impinged upon his economic interests. The Chamber of Commerce urged enactment of the 1906 ordinance in order "to increase our industrial prosperity." "With the palls of smoke which darken our sky continually and the almost continuous deposits of soot," the Chamber explained, "our dirty streets and grimy buildings are simply evidences of the difficulty under which we labor in any endeavor to present Pittsburgh as an ideal home city."[12]

Following passage of the smoke ordinance, a Division of Smoke Inspection was created in the Bureau of Health in 1907; at the request of the mayor, the Chamber helped select the chief smoke inspector.[13] The courts declared the ordinance unconstitutional in

than 20 percent dense smoke for over three minutes, but it was voided by the courts. This account is drawn from *Some Engineering Phases of Pittsburgh's Smoke Problem,* Mellon Institute of Industrial Research and School of Specific Industries, Smoke Investigation, *Bulletin No. 8* (University of Pittsburgh, 1914), 11–15.

[11] *What Has the Chamber of Commerce done?* (n.d., n.p.); Pittsburgh Chamber of Commerce, *Fifty Years of the Chamber of Commerce of Pittsburgh, 1874–1924* (Pittsburgh, 1924), 74. The 1906 ordinance prohibited dense black or gray smoke from any chimney or smokestack in connection with any furnace, heating, power or manufacturing plant, locomotive, motor vehicle, apartment house, office building, hotel, theater, school, or factory. Private residences were exempted, and the provisions were suspended if it could be demonstrated that there was no practical device to prevent the emission of dense black or gray smoke. Violators were subject to fines of $10 to $100 for each day of the violation.

[12] Pittsburgh Chamber of Commerce, "Report of Committee on Municipal Affairs, October 29, 1906," in Municipal Record, *Minutes of the Proceedings of the Select Council of the City of Pittsburgh, For the Year 1906–1907,* Vol. 39, 210.

[13] *A Year's Record of Great Achievements. Annual Report of the President to the Chamber of Commerce of Pittsburgh, May, 1908,* 23. The first Chief Smoke Inspector was William H. Rea, who headed a force of three inspectors.

1911 on the grounds that the city council had exceeded its authority, and that the measure was unreasonable. The state legislature promptly passed enabling legislation, and a new ordinance was enacted (which exempted mill heating and puddling furnaces).[14] In 1912 the Chamber organized a Smoke and Dust Abatement League to support the work of the Division of Smoke Inspection (which was elevated to a Bureau of Smoke Regulation in 1914).[15] Another assault against smoke was launched in 1911 when Robert Duncan Kennedy, a Pittsburgh businessman, provided funds to the Mellon Institute of the University of Pittsburgh for research. Under its sponsorship, scientists explored the economic costs, health hazards, and psychological consequences of a smoky atmosphere.[16]

Business and scientific interest in smoke control, and the crea-

[14] Ralph G. Herman, "Regulation of Smoke and Air Pollution in Pennsylvania," *University of Pittsburgh Law Review*, 10 (1948–1949), 495; City of Pittsburgh, Department of Public Health, *Annual Report, 1911*, 307; "What the Chamber of Commerce Has Achieved," 35 (cited in footnote 10).

[15] The Smoke and Dust Abatement League was composed of the Allegheny County Medical Society; Oakland Board of Trade; Civic Club; Twentieth Century Club; Carnegie Institute of Technology; Consumers' League of Western Pennsylvania; Chamber of Commerce; and University of Pittsburgh. (*Pittsburgh Post*, November 23, 1913; *Pittsburgh Bulletin*, November, 1913.) During its first year the League conducted exhibits at the Western Pennsylvania Exposition and East Liberty Exposition; it was responsible for the creation of the Bureau of Smoke Regulation and a revised smoke ordinance in 1914. (*Pittsburgh Post*, December 5, 1913; *Pittsburgh Gazette Times*, October 8, 1916.) The revised ordinance of 1914 limited the emission of dense smoke to one minute in any eight minute period for steamboats and locomotives, and two minutes in any fifteen minute period for stationary stacks.

[16] Between 1912 and 1914, the University of Pittsburgh published nine bulletins on the smoke problem for the Mellon Institute of Industrial Research and School of Specific Industries. They included: *Outline of the Smoke Investigation* (1912); Ellwood H. McClelland, *Bibliography of Smoke and Smoke Prevention* (1913); J. E. Wallace Wallin, *Psychological Aspects of the Problem of Atmospheric Smoke Pollution* (1913); John J. O'Connor, Jr., *The Economic Cost of the Smoke Nuisance to Pittsburgh* (1913); Herbert H. Kimball, *The Meteorological Aspects of the Smoke Problem* (1913); Raymond C. Benner (ed.), *Papers on the Effect of Smoke on Building Materials* (1913); J. F. Clevenger, *The Effect of the Soot in Smoke on Vegetation* (1913); *Some Engineering Phases of Pittsburgh's Smoke Problem* (1914); O. Klotz and Wm. Charles White, *Papers on the Influence of Smoke and Health* (1914).

Point, early twentieth century.

tion of a municipal regulatory machinery, had no perceptible results. Businessmen had to use government to extend their influence in civic affairs, but did not really want government power to compromise their autonomy. In smoke control, as in housing, they could reconcile these incompatible goals by creating a public bureaucracy with a feeble regulatory mandate and no constructive powers of intervention. Even the staunchest advocate of smoke control conceded that it would have to be sacrificed in the event of a conflict with local economic interests. The Civic Club, for one, "would be the last to advocate the passage of any law which would tend to lessen our prosperity." Legislation for the "many" was, according to the Congress of Women's Clubs of Allegheny County, permissible so long as their interests "can be subserved without . . . affecting the material prosperity of which we are all so justly proud."[17] Unfortunately, smoke control could not be both effective and absolutely painless for all economic interests involved. Recognizing its ambiguous status, the Division of Smoke Inspection, like its housing counterparts, adopted a strategy of education and persuasion.

[17] Municipal Record, *Minutes of the Proceedings of the Select Council of the City of Pittsburgh, For the Year 1906–1907*, Vol. 39, 210.

The chief smoke inspector noted that the tendency in Pittsburgh to equate smoke with prosperity inspired criticism of any regulatory legislation. It was, however, surely not the "purpose of the City of Pittsburgh . . . to harass or drive away the resident mill or factory operator," or to discourage the "prospective investor and manufacturer."[18] In compliance with this policy, the Division rarely prosecuted offenders.[19] It drove no manufacturer from Pittsburgh; neither did it reduce the volume of smoke by a wisp.

An important exception to the rule that public agencies were to perform a predominantly regulatory function occurred in recreation and park development. In this area of environmental change, no private economic prerogative was challenged. This legitimized constructive governmental intervention. Bureaucratic rationalization was fully compatible with public decision making and substantive power.

Municipal responsibility in Pittsburgh for recreational and play facilities evolved from the summer playground opened by the Civic Club in 1896. The experiment was initiated by Beulah Kennard, chairman of the Club's Department of Education.[20] In 1899 the Board of Education began to contribute funds toward maintenance of the 12 playgrounds in operation. In collaboration with the women's clubs of Allegheny County, the work was expanded in 1900 to include vacation schools. The joint supervisory committee split into a Pittsburgh and Allegheny branch in 1904; and in 1906 the Pittsburgh group reorganized as the Pittsburgh Recreation Association. Its second superintendent, W. F.

[18] City of Pittsburgh, Department of Public Health, Division of Smoke Inspection, *Annual Report, 1910,* 214; City of Pittsburgh, Department of Public Health, Bureau of Smoke Regulation, *Annual Report, 1915,* in *Annual Reports of Departments and Offices of the City of Pittsburgh, 1915,* 239.

[19] City of Pittsburgh, *Report on a Survey of the Department of Public Health, Prepared for the City Council by the New York Bureau of Municipal Research, June–July, 1913,* 25. World War I further hampered enforcement, and by 1917 the bureau was charged "with inefficiency and lack of courage to bring prosecutions justified by existing conditions." (*Pittsburgh Press,* November 25, 1917).

[20] *An Historical Report of the Bureau of Recreation, Pittsburgh, Pa., Recording Six Years' Work, 1916–1921,* 7.

Ashe, became director of the new Bureau of Recreation, established by the city in 1915. The Bureau took over the playgrounds and recreation centers, except in the North Side where the Allegheny Playground Association proved "unwilling to undergo municipalization."[21]

Public recreation posed no threat to private economic prerogatives, and had positive advantages as a social control mechanism. It was a conservative mode of environmental improvement, one that appealed to the social worker and businessman as a means toward Americanization, good citizenship, and industrial peace. Through supervised play activity, the child's "moral nature" could be developed. Neither school, home, nor street could provide all the "necessities of life and growth," or cope with the European who "comes to us as raw material needing much social training and discipline to fit him for the responsibilities of American citizenship." The "play spirit" was nothing less than the "common denominator of the future." It was the path to "civic unity," nurturing the "bond of fellowship that shall make the common interests of the poor, the rich, the wage earners paramount to the competitive war which sets them in opposing and jealous camps."[22]

The same logic applied to the parks movement. One of the singular achievements of the post-Civil War decades in Pittsburgh and other cities was the creation of their public park systems. These greatly expanded the scope of municipal service and welfare functions, and constituted an important root of comprehensive city planning ideals.[23] A single public official was largely responsible for park development in Pittsburgh.

Edward M. Bigelow, a native Pittsburgher, was born in 1850. He attended the Western University of Pennsylvania (later Uni-

[21] Ibid., 7–9; W. F. Ashe, "Pittsburgh Playgrounds," Survey, 45 (February 26, 1921), 768.

[22] Beulah Kennard, "Pittsburgh's Experience With Summer Playgrounds," Chautauquan, 36 (November 1902), 197; Beulah Kennard, "Pittsburgh's Playgrounds," Survey, 22 (May 1, 1909), 195, 196.

[23] Roy Lubove, "H. W. S. Cleveland and the Urban-Rural Continuum in American Landscape Architecture," in Lubove (ed.), H. W. S. Cleveland, Landscape Architecture as Applied to the Wants of the West (Pittsburgh: University of Pittsburgh Press, 1965), vii-xxi.

versity of Pittsburgh) and became a civil engineer. Appointed
City Engineer in 1880, Bigelow became director of the Department of Public Works upon its creation in 1889. He remained in
this post until 1900, was reappointed in 1903, and in 1906 became state highway commissioner. The main responsibilities of
Bigelow's Department included surveys, roads, sewers, water
supply, and street lighting. In park planning and development,
Bigelow grasped an opportunity for constructive environmental
intervention that did not exist in other phases of the Department's work (or in municipal government as a whole). Frequently, the DPW could act only in response to the initiative of
private property owners and developers. In response to criticism
of the "deplorable condition of the mud streets," for example,
Bigelow explained that the department could not pave them of
its own volition. Property owners had to petition for the improvement, which then had to be approved by council ordinance.[24]

A precedent for Bigelow's park schemes was the Common
Ground Improvement Act of 1867, which authorized Allegheny
to develop its Common as a public park and establish a park
commission.[25] Bigelow requested the Pittsburgh city council to
appoint a Committee on Parks in 1889. This led to ordinances
setting aside ground around Herron Hill and Highland reservoirs
for parks, and authorizing the DPW to maintain them. Bigelow
also played an important role in the negotiations in 1889 which
led to Mary Schenley's donation of sevaral hundred acres for a
park.[26] Bigelow viewed 1889 as a watershed in Pittsburgh's
history. When the "money was being piled up" in the past, the
citizens "seemed to have clothed themselves in sordidness."
Recognition of the value of "breathing spots for the people"
inaugurated a new era of aesthetic and social consciousness.[27]
Until 1900 Bigelow was not only the "mastermind behind the
schemes of the acquisition of grounds, but in a large measure
was actually responsible for physical development." In 1896 he

[24] City of Pittsburgh, Department of Public Works, *Annual Report, 1889*, 12.
[25] Ralph E. Griswold, "Wright was Wrong," *Landscape Architecture*, 53
(April 1963), 210.
[26] Howard Stewart (ed.), *Historical Data: Pittsburgh Public Parks* (Pittsburgh: Greater Pittsburgh Parks Association, 1943), iii.
[27] City of Pittsburgh, Department of Public Works, *Annual Report, 1889*, 17.

brought William Falconer, a professional park planner, to Pittsburgh as his assistant.[28] Between them the early city park system was designed in the romantic, naturalistic idiom of Andrew Jackson Downing and the English country estate.

The extension of the municipal planning function from parks to the broader physical environment occurred in 1911, when an official City Planning Commission was established. This marked the climax of the thrust toward bureaucratic rationalization. Decision making was centralized in a single mechanism that touched on every aspect of the environment. Yet city planning had to be adapted to the prerogatives of private interest groups. Their autonomy had to be reconciled somehow with the concentration of authority in a public agency. What happened, in fact, was the delegation to the city planning commission of unlimited authority to engage in research and to proffer advice, and a single, negative regulatory function. Equally important, the Commission, as the embodiment of the "public interest," was detached from the municipal political and bureaucratic power structure. It was an administrative eunuch—independent, uncontaminated, and thoroughly impotent.

Like other reforms, city planning in Pittsburgh was initiated by a business-professional elite. The prime mover, in this case, was the Civic Commission. The Pittsburgh Survey provided an important stimulus. "Certain citizens," according to the Commission, saw "in such an investigation a basis of adequate information for the most fundamental and comprehensive future advance ever yet made possible in America. Plans could be framed and support secured for improvements on a scale commensurate with the scope and thoroughness of the Survey."[29] One of the Commission's first acts was to select Bion J. Arnold of Chicago, John R. Freeman of Providence, and Frederick Law Olmsted of Boston to prepare a city planning report.

Completed and adopted by the Civic Commission late in 1909, it was essentially an outline of study areas: steam railroads, water transportation, flood protection, electric railroads, streets, public buildings, water and sewerage, smoke control, regulation of pri-

---

[28] Stewart, *Historical Data*, iii, iv.
[29] Pittsburgh Civic Commission, *Plan and Scope* (n.p., n.d.).

vate property, and building code revision.[30] The report, among
the first general planning documents in Pittsburgh, led mostly to
other studies.[31] Mayor Magee requested Arnold to proceed with
studies of the electric and steam railroads, and he secured Allen
Hazen of New York to investigate the sewerage system. The
Civic Commission retained Olmsted to prepare a downtown and
main thoroughfare plan.

The Commission adopted Olmsted's plan in December, 1910.
It went beyond detailed proposals for streets and a downtown
civic center. Olmsted stressed the need for accurate topographical
data as a basis for planning, especially in Pittsburgh with its
"difficult complication of high ridges, deep valleys, and precipitous slopes." Although the Bureau of Surveys in the Department
of Public Works had to inform the council of every subdivision
proposal, it never had the funds to acquire the information "upon
which *alone* such a report could be intelligently based."[32] Olmsted's most imaginative recommendations included a constructive
municipal policy toward steep-slope land. Comprising more than
25 percent of the city land area, these slopes were haphazardly
developed, expensive to service, and often delinquent in taxes.
He suggested that the city acquire such land and convert it from
a public nuisance into an aesthetic and park asset. These proposals, and others for beautification and recreational use of the
extensive waterfronts, were ignored at the time but revived after
1945.

In its campaign for city planning, as well as for tax reform, the
Civic Commission found an ally in Mayor Magee—a combina-

[30] Pittsburgh Civic Commission, *City Planning for Pittsburgh. Outline and
Procedure. A Report by Bion J. Arnold, Chicago, John R. Freeman, Providence, Frederick Law Olmsted, Boston* (adopted by the Commission,
December 1909) (Pittsburgh, June 1910).
[31] Charles Mulford Robinson, a landscape architect, had prepared a planning study for the Pittsburgh Survey the same year. See Charles Mulford
Robinson, "Civic Improvement Possibilities of Pittsburgh," *Charities and
the Commons*, 21 (February 6, 1909), 801–26.
[32] Pittsburgh Civic Commission, *Pittsburgh: Main Thoroughfares and the
Downtown District. Improvements Necessary to Meet the City's Present
and Future Needs. A Report by Frederick Law Olmsted, Prepared under
the Direction of the Committee on City Planning* (Adopted by the Commission, December, 1910) (Pittsburgh, 1911), 93, 94.

tion of machine politician and social statesman somewhat reminiscent of Alfred E. Smith. Magee settled for city planning in
lieu of metropolitan government. He had supported a Greater
Pittsburgh act in the state legislative session of 1911, which
would have annexed 40 surrounding communities. "Some form of
centralized administration is . . . necessary," he insisted. Planning,
realistically, had to encompass the metropolitan area in order to
deal with problems such as air pollution, highways, water, and
waste disposal. If metropolitan government could not be achieved
through annexation, he favored the metropolitan district scheme
used in London and Boston.[33]

Advocates of city planning, like the mayor, described it as the
assertion of the "public interest" in contrast to the "individual
interest." In pursuing the public interest it "strives for the ideal"
and "an abstract conception of the future." It was necessary,
therefore, to organize the city planning commission as a "separate and independent body" that could resist particularistic pressures. As a detached, disinterested advocate of the general
interest, it was the logical coordinating agency for the entire
community. Substituting rational priorities for expediency, it
would channel "all the forces of growth and progress . . . into
one co-ordinated plan."[34]

This formulation had no relation to political or institutional
reality. In the first place, the Commission's substantive powers
were trivial. The 1911 legislation created a Department of City
Planning in second-class cities under the control of a nine-
member commission appointed by the mayor. It had three advisory functions and one regulatory power. All ordinances introduced into the city council concerning the location of public
projects had to be transmitted to the Commission for study and
recommendation. The Commission was authorized to prepare a
map or maps constituting the city plan. And it could transmit advice on physical development to any individual or public agency.
Its one power was approval of all private subdivision plans as a
prerequisite to official recording.[35]

[33] City of Pittsburgh, *Annual Reports of the Executive Departments For
the Year Ending January 31, 1912*, I, 12, 13, 60, 62.
[34] *Ibid.*, 58, 64.
[35] For the Assembly Act creating the Commission, see City of Pittsburgh,

Even if the Commission possessed greater statutory powers, it would have been debilitated by its anomalous administrative status. The planning function was disemboweled from the start. As an independent body, the Commission was isolated from politics, but it was also isolated from political leverage. It was an administrative *objet d'art* with no place in the municipal power structure. The public interest resolves itself into a multiplicity of competing public and private interest groups, and ultimately into a process of political decision making in which the Commission had no voice.

The City Planning Commission considered its chief tasks to be the preparation of a city plan and service to the community as a "clearing house of all civic effort."[36] In reality, proposals for road and subdivision improvements occupied most of its attention. And hardly was the Commission established before it was dismantled as part of Mayor Armstrong's economy drive. The Department's professional staff was eliminated except for a "Secretary-Engineer," shared with the Department of Public Works.[37] After 1918, the planning vacuum would be filled, in part, by a voluntary Citizens' Committee on the City Plan.

The City Planning Commission was supposed to concern itself with practical affairs. A Municipal Art Commission, also established in 1911, would deal with the "City Beautiful." Advocated by the art committee of the Civic Commission and modeled after the art commissions of Boston and New York, the Pittsburgh agency consisted of nine members appointed by the mayor.[38] Its only power was a veto over any art work acquired by the city, the design of city buildings, and other construction; but it anticipated that civic beautification would result more from its educational efforts than use of the veto. Like the Planning Commission,

Department of City Planning, *Annual Report, 1912,* in City of Pittsburgh, *Annual Report of the Executive Departments, Year Ending January 31, 1913,* 149–151.

[36] *Ibid.,* 162, 163.

[37] City of Pittsburgh, *Annual Reports of Departments and Offices, 1914,* xi.

[38] Supporting the Civic Commission's proposal for an Art Commission were the Civic Club, Pittsburgh Art Society, and Beautification Committee of the Greater Pittsburgh Association. *An Account of the Work of the Art Commission of the City of Pittsburgh. From its Creation in 1911 to January 1st, 1915,* 7.

it had unlimited power to provide advice to citizens or public agencies. The Art Commission's most ambitious project was the improvement of Pittsburgh's Point. It employed a Chicago architect-planner, E. H. Bennett, to prepare a study—one of the first in a long series of proposals to redevelop this area (culminating in Point Park and Gateway Center after World War II). However, the Bennett report, earnestly endorsed by the Art Commission, had no impact at the time.[39]

The Municipal Art Commission helped keep the city planning idea alive in Pittsburgh during the indifferent years of the Armstrong administration. Its broad perspective was attributable, in part, to the influence of Frederick Bigger, an architect appointed assistant secretary in 1914 and Pittsburgh's leading professional planner during the interwar decades. The Art Commission maintained that beautification could not be achieved without "attention . . . to the fundamental city planning ideas." These provided the "basis of civic orderliness which is of fundamental value to the work an art commission is called upon to do." As early as 1917 the Art Commission called for a zoning act.[40] Passed in 1923, it helped revive the moribund city planning department.

In its key aspects—housing, city planning, smoke control, and taxation—the quest for environmental regeneration in Pittsburgh failed. It had been identified with a business and professional elite whose ideal of bureaucratic rationalization was compromised by a reluctance to encroach upon the prerogatives of voluntary interests. The public sector did acquire new powers, but constructive responsibility for generating change remained

[39] For the Bennett Report, completed in 1914, see City of Pittsburgh, Art Commission, *Annual Report, 1914,* in City of Pittsburgh, *Annual Reports of Departments and Offices, 1914,* 11ff. The principal recommendations included construction of a South Point bridge and a Duquesne Way approach. The Art Commission complained that the "importance of the project for securing a comprehensive and proper plan for the Point district failed to be generally appreciated to the extent of securing enthusiastic cooperation, and the Commission found itself meeting with failure and discouragement in its efforts along these lines." *An Account of the Work of the Art Commission,* 42.

[40] City of Pittsburgh, Art Commission, *Annual Report, 1916,* in City of Pittsburgh, *Annual Reports of Departments and Offices, 1916,* 30; City of Pittsburgh, Art Commission, *Annual Report, 1917,* 6.

under private auspices. As a consequence, decision making was not centralized to the degree required to effect significant change. In housing, for example, the small entrepreneur rather than the large-scale, nonspeculative housing company continued to dominate the market. Housing conditions in Pittsburgh during the interwar decades demonstrated vividly the inadequacy of the early twentieth century reform program.

FOUR

Housing: The Gordian Knot

The old journalistic pastime—who could find Pittsburgh most repulsive and why—flourished between the wars. Pittsburgh would have emerged as the envy of America if scabrous criticism alone could reconstruct a city. H. L. Mencken, for one, peered through the smog and detected a "scene so dreadfully hideous, so intolerably bleak and forlorn that it reduced the whole aspiration of man to a macabre and depressing joke. . . . I am not speaking of mere filth. One expects steel towns to be dirty. What I allude to is the unbroken and agonizing ugliness, the sheer revolting monstrousness, of every house in sight."[1]

Others were more distressed by the intellectual and cultural blight. "The supreme crime in Pittsburgh," according to R. L. Duffus, was "willful defiance of the little group of Scotch-Presbyterians who regard themselves as having been elected by Providence to be the city's masters, and who are, in fact, its masters." Their economic and religious values had produced a civilization which was "dull" at best, and otherwise "barbaric." The city would benefit immeasurably from "one large and comprehensive funeral—it needs to bury John Calvin so deep that he will never get up again."[2] Dwight Macdonald conjured up the same image of a "big-business culture at its crudest and most powerful," tempered by a "veneer of spirituality." Nowhere were the worldly needs of the average citizen more neglected, and nowhere was there a more "anxious concern" for his spiritual

---

[1] Quoted in Stefan Lorant, *Pittsburgh: The Story of an American City* (Garden City, New York: Doubleday, 1964), 328.
[2] R. L. Duffus, "Is Pittsburgh Civilized?", *Harper's Magazine*, 161 (October 1930), 537, 545.

welfare. Richard B. Mellon, brother of Treasury Secretary Andrew Mellon, had responded magnificently to the "challenge of the depression in 1931 by announcing a gift of $4,000,000 to build the East Liberty Presbyterian Church."[3]

Macdonald singled out the Hearst Press and John G. Bowman, Chancellor of the University of Pittsburgh, as the leading prophets of the local business culture. Bowman did tend to rhapsodize over Pittsburgh business genius. "Business insight was developed here as the drama, for example, was developed in London at the time of Elizabeth."[4] Among his dubious contributions to higher education was a notorious assault upon academic freedom, which culminated in the dismissal of the historian Ralph E. Turner in 1934. By this time, "suppression of liberal activities and the dismissal of teachers who manifest even the faintest pink hue have occurred at the University of Pittsburgh so often that they have ceased to be news."[5]

A latter-day Pittsburgh Survey, published in 1938, confirmed the journalistic diagnoses. More limited in scope than the original Survey, the *Social Study of Pittsburgh* focused on social welfare issues.[6] It found the local agencies to be neither innovative, efficient, nor geared to social action. The "dominant public opinion" that controlled social work practice was shaped by the "economic hegemony of the industrial and financial corporations; by the conservative and, in important places, fundamentalist

[3] Dwight Macdonald, "Pittsburgh: What a City Shouldn't Be," *Forum*, **100** (August 1938), 51, 57, 56.

[4] John G. Bowman, "Pittsburgh's Contribution to Civilization," in *Pittsburgh and the Pittsburgh Spirit: Addresses at the Chamber of Commerce of Pittsburgh, 1927–1928* (Pittsburgh: Pittsburgh Chamber of Commerce, 1928), 9.

[5] Rose M. Stein, "Academic Cossacks in Pittsburgh," *Nation*, **141** (July 24, 1935), 105.

[6] Philip Klein, et al., *A Social Study of Pittsburgh: Community Problems and Social Services of Allegheny County* (New York: Columbia University Press, 1938). The proposal for the social study was originally made by the Pittsburgh Welfare Fund which, in collaboration with the Federation of Social Agencies, requested financial support from the Buhl Foundation. A joint committee of the two agencies selected seven citizens and comprised the Citizens' Committee of the Social Study of Pittsburgh and Allegheny County, official sponsor of the investigation. (*Survey Graphic*, **27** (February 1938), 133.)

theology of the leading local denominations." Dissent was "little tolerated" in this atmosphere of militant orthodoxy.[7] A key element of the Pittsburgh creed was the superiority of the western European heritage (or, as Macdonald had put it, "the general idea is that the Hunkies were brought to Pittsburgh by the Almighty . . . to do the dirty work, to accept low wages, and to keep their months shut").[8] The employers and rich, in short, were the natural leaders of the community; and their reign was sanctified by the "pervasive veneration of property and of the legal structure."[9] The industrial and financial leadership maintained ultimate control over the social welfare program through economic leverage and board membership. A survey of 1288 board members of Community Fund agencies revealed that their contributions amounted to one-third of agency income in 1934; another 23 percent came from corporations.[10]

Elite sponsorship and denominational organization had produced a conservative social work system that actually discriminated against the two groups most in need of services—the immigrant and the Negro. This embodied the "greatest and bitterest paradox of social work and the severest reflection upon its voluntary sponsorship." In social work, as in higher education, any challenge to orthodoxy evoked swift reprisals. The authors of the *Social Study of Pittsburgh* were impressed by the dismissal in 1935 of the YMCA secretary. His sympathetic attitude toward use of agency facilities for discussion of radical social programs had apparently distressed large donors and the Hearst *Sun-Telegraph*.[11]

Social critics of Pittsburgh were absorbed by the role of a conservative elite in directing or, more likely, inhibiting change. Few recognized that a decisive change, dating back to at least 1910,

---

[7] Klein, *Social Study of Pittsburgh*, 290.

[8] Macdonald, "Pittsburgh," 52.

[9] Klein, *Social Study of Pittsburgh*, 290.

[10] *Ibid.*, 363. For all practical purposes, "the control of practically the entire body of voluntary social work rests in the hands of some 1,300 persons consisting, with negligible exceptions, of the representatives of industrial and financial control, the wealthy minority characterized by the greatest conservatism in political, economic, and social philosophy" (p. 364).

[11] *Ibid.*, 400, 912–913.

was in progress and would, in the long run, profoundly influence the response to community problems. The authors of the Pittsburgh Survey had emphasized the need for modernization of governmental and social institutions; parity had to be achieved with the industrial sector in terms of efficiency, centralization, and planning. They could not realize that Pittsburgh was on the verge of a long period of economic decline, and that the industrial sector would develop many of the same rigidities and archaisms attributed to social institutions. The nineteenth century had been a period of creative response to locational advantages and contemporary technology, but Pittsburgh's economy would remain in the nineteenth century despite changing technological and market circumstances.

By 1910 the key feature of the regional economy was the concentration of the labor force in the large plants or production units associated with a limited range of heavy industries: coal, iron and steel, electrical equipment, and glass. Large-plant concentration and overspecialization inhibited adaptation to twentieth century economic trends. One problem was the huge capital investment in existing facilities. Another was the fact that Pittsburgh's heavy industry concentration did not provide the external economies that gestate large numbers of small suppliers, businesses, and services.[12] By the Second World War, Pittsburgh had become a classic case of the mature industrial area, characterized by a decline in the growth rates of heavy industry, total production, employment, and population.[13]

Comparatively favorable growth rates in glass, electrical equip-

---

[12] See the three volumes of the *Economic Study of the Pittsburgh Region* (conducted by the Pittsburgh Regional Planning Association) (Pittsburgh: University of Pittsburgh Press, 1963). A good summary statement is by Edgar M. Hoover, "Pittsburgh Takes Stock of Itself," in Benjamin Chinitz (ed.), *City and Suburb: The Economics of Metropolitan Growth* (Englewood Cliffs, New Jersey: Prentice-Hall, 1964), 53–65. "The region," Hoover explains, "primarily by virtue of its specialization in types of industry involving very large plants and very large firms, has a notably smaller complement and variety of the kinds of supporting services upon which small and new firms are particularly dependent" (p. 57).

[13] Glenn E. McLaughlin and Ralph J. Watkins, "The Problem of Industrial Growth in a Mature Economy," *American Economic Review*, 29 (March 1939), Pt. 2, supplement, 2.

ment, and aluminum could not compensate for the dramatic downward trends in coal and steel after 1910. At the same time, no "new major industry" took root after 1900; indeed, no important industry that emerged in the twentieth century significantly influenced economic development in the Pittsburgh region. Unemployment had become a problem before the great depression. It reached 5 to 10 percent of the labor force in 1929.[14] The sluggishness of the economy was reflected in a sharp drop in the rate of population growth over most of the twentieth century.[15]

These general economic trends necessarily influenced the process of environmental change. "One of the major problems of industrial maturity is likely to be the shortage of capital for improving social conditions. Many social and government problems created during the boom stage of development have been left for solution in the stage of industrial maturity—when the cost can be least afforded."[16] Housing, during the growth era, had fared badly in the competition for capital; after World War I, the financing problem was vastly complicated by the economic decline. At the same time, inflationary pressures raised housing costs to a permanently high plateau and speculative builders withdrew from the low-income housing market. These developments contributed to shortages and deterioration of the housing

[14] Glenn E. McLaughlin, *Growth of American Manufacturing Areas: A Comparative Analysis with Special Emphasis on Trends in the Pittsburgh District* (Pittsburgh: University of Pittsburgh, Bureau of Business Research Monographs, No. 7, 1938), 316; McLaughlin and Watkins, "The Problem of Industrial Growth in a Mature Economy," 11.

[15] Between 1880–1910, Allegheny County increased in population from 355,869 to more than 1 million; percentage increases by decade were, respectively, 55.1, 40.4, and 31.4. The City of Pittsburgh, during the same period, increased in population from 156,389 to 533,905; percentage increases, by decade, were 52.6, 34.8, and 66.0. Growth rates for the decades 1910–1940 contrasted sharply. During this thirty-year period, Allegheny County's population rose to 1,411,539; expressed in percentages, by decade, the figures are 16.4, 15.9, and 2.7. The population of the City of Pittsburgh in 1940 was 671,659; its percentage increases from 1910–1940, by decade, were 10.2, 13.8, and 0.3. Bertram J. Black and Aubrey Mallach, *Population Trends in Allegheny County, 1840–1943* (Pittsburgh: Bureau of Social Research, Federation of Social Agencies, 1944), 2.

[16] McLaughlin and Watkins, "The Problem of Industrial Growth in a Mature Economy," 13 (cited in footnote 13).

stock, which reached crisis proportions during the early 1920's and throughout the 1930's.

Despite new conditions, the early twentieth century pattern of elite, voluntary reform persisted. Social orthodoxy in Pittsburgh did not imply indifference to welfare problems or uncompromising resistance to change; it implied, instead, a reform program formulated by business and professional leaders, conceived in relation to business interests, and executed largely by voluntary agencies. It became increasingly apparent by the depression that mass housing betterment under voluntary auspices was less a social policy than a substitute for one.

The housing crisis following World War I had alarmed the Pittsburgh Chamber of Commerce. Compounded of shortages, rising construction costs and spiraling rents, it was the most serious in the nation's history and a threat to the community's future.[17] Pittsburgh could not compete against industrial areas that provided superior housing accommodations. Her "prosperity and growth" depended upon "prompt action to provide adequate housing." Yet responsibility could not be delegated to government at any level. It belonged to "some strong and impartial civic organization, representing all interests"—like the Chamber of Commerce.[18] Following the appointment of a Special Housing Committee in January, 1921, the Chamber organized a Commerce Housing Corporation to help relieve the housing shortage.

[17] The national housing crisis during and after World War I is discussed in Roy Lubove, *Community Planning in the 1920's: The Contribution of the Regional Planning Association of America* (Pittsburgh: University of Pittsburgh Press, 1963), 17–22.

[18] W. H. Walker, "A Housing Plan for City of Pittsburgh," *Pittsburgh First*, 1 (January 31, 1920), 8. As late as June, 1926, "rents of workers' dwellings in Pittsburgh" were 75.4 percent above the December, 1917 level, the sharpest increase having occurred between 1917 and 1921. In 1932 they were still 35.9 percent above the December, 1917 level. Construction costs also experienced a sharp and permanent rise. Taking 1917 as the norm, the index had risen to 169 in 1920. It dropped to 126 by 1922, but recovered in 1923 and fluctuated between 136 and 142 until 1930. If 1913 is used as the base, construction costs in 1929 were 95 percent higher. See Theodore A. Veenstra, "Real Estate Finance in Allegheny County—The Statistical Position," *Pittsburgh Business Review*, 2 (October 1932), 13–16. Also, Joseph M. Gillman, *Rent Levels in Pittsburgh, Pennsylvania, and Their Causes* (Pittsburgh: University of Pittsburgh, 1926).

The Chamber hoped that by demonstrating methods of erecting low-cost homes it would provide an inspiration to investors and builders.[19] Between 1921 and 1924 the Corporation was responsible for the construction of 304 houses in Allegheny County. The Chamber Housing Corporation not only faded away after three years and a token contribution to the housing supply, but it lost nearly $12,000 in the process.[20] Its inspirational value was dubious.

The Chamber Housing Corporation was more significant for what it represented than for what it accomplished. It was another example of the extent to which planned environmental intervention hinged upon the initiative of business leaders, who attempted to extend their influence through voluntary civic association. Pittsburgh, however, lagged behind other major cities in establishing a community-wide citizens' agency to deal with housing. It was not until 1928 that the Chamber of Commerce, Civic Club, and Federation of Social Agencies helped launch the Pittsburgh Housing Association.[21] Its first director, John Ihlder, was impressed by one contrast between 1928 and 1921, when the Chamber of Commerce established its Housing Corporation. He shaped the Association's early program on the assumption that the housing shortage had been overcome and a substantial vacancy rate existed.[22]

[19] "Report of the Committee on Housing," *Pittsburgh First*, 3 (May 28, 1921), 3–4; "Development of Commerce Housing Corporation," *Pittsburgh First*, 3 (December 31, 1921), 26. The Commerce Housing Corporation provided a "complete housing service, which included the providing of plans and specifications, the taking of bids and the letting of contracts, the inspection of materials and construction to completion." (*Ibid.*)

[20] Lester Bernstein, "Commerce Housing Corporation Dissolved—Most Successful Undertaking Formally Terminated," *Greater Pittsburgh*, 8 (January 1, 1927), 1–2; Pittsburgh Housing Association, *Housing in Pittsburgh, First Annual Report, October 1st, 1928 to December 31st, 1929* (with Supplementary Material to May 1st, 1930). The Commerce Housing Corporation was legally dissolved in 1926.

[21] *The Federator*, 3 (November 1928), 4; Klein, et al., *A Social Study of Pittsburgh*, 222 (cited in footnote 6).

[22] Ihlder was a veteran housing reformer. He had been associated with Lawrence Veiller in the early twentieth century as field director of the National Housing Association. He then became director of the Philadelphia Housing Association (upon which the Pittsburgh organization was mod-

Pittsburgh builders, Ihlder maintained, were meeting the effective demand for new dwellings. The new housing, admittedly, fell "beyond the means of that part of the population whose need is greatest. Even building at a loss would not reach these people in sufficient amount to be of any effect."[23] The high vacancy rate was a key to the widespread improvement of housing conditions despite the withdrawal of the speculative developer from the low-income market. A sufficient supply of good, low-cost housing could be assured through the rehabilitation of substandard vacant dwellings in addition to the rehabilitation and conservation of occupied low-rent units.[24] Widespread rehabilitation of the existing housing stock would be achieved, presumably, through intensive code enforcement. Ihlder was confident that "enforcement of the legal standards" would not only provide more housing at less cost than new construction, but would in time liberate Pittsburgh from its blighted areas.[25]

Ihlder complained of two circumstances, peculiar to Pittsburgh, that inhibited efforts to cope with the widespread "rotten bad housing." He described one as a "very real inferiority complex" that nurtured a fatalistic attitude toward community problems. Sensationalist agitation and publicity would either reinforce the sense of hopelessness or produce resentment. The Association, therefore, should adopt the "more difficult inspiration method."[26] A second problem revolved around the difficulty of acquiring the most elementary data. Public agencies in Pittsburgh were, to say the least, informal about the publication of reports. The fact that no city department reports had appeared since 1916 was a "surprise and . . . somewhat of a mystery." Ihlder had expected

---

eled), and served for eight years as manager of the Civic Development Department of the U. S. Chamber of Commerce.

[23] "Report of Executive Director," Board of Directors Meeting, October 2, 1929, Pittsburgh Housing Association, Minutes. These Minutes are part of the files of ACTION-Housing.

[24] *Ibid.*; Pittsburgh Housing Association, *Housing in Pittsburgh, First Annual Report, October 1st, 1928 to December 31st, 1929*, 5–6.

[25] *Ibid.*, 6; John Ihlder, *Better Dwellings: Work of the Pittsburgh Housing Association* (n.p., n.d.).

[26] Memo from John Ihlder to Eleanor S. Webster, August 15, 1929; "Executive Director's Report to the Board of Directors, March 21, 1929," Pittsburgh Housing Association, Minutes.

to receive systematic complaints from health and welfare agencies about substandard housing, but discovered that their workers did not know what was illegal. The sanitary and housing code had not been reprinted since 1913 and only three known copies existed. Ihlder had the impression "that some people fear that facts may be to the discredit of Pittsburgh."[27]

Problems of civic morale or data were comparatively marginal. Other factors would determine whether "better housing is primarily a matter of law and law enforcement."[28] As suggested in a previous chapter, code enforcement is largely futile in the absence of a housing surplus that can compensate for the demolition of unfit dwellings, or an increase in costs and rentals resulting from rehabilitation. Thus Ihlder's strategy of rehabilitation through code enforcement hinged, in large measure, upon the existence of a high vacancy rate in the late 1920's. As it turned out, this policy had little validity because it was based upon an ephemeral circumstance. The depression soon struck and code enforcement had little relevance to such problems as squatter colonies, evictions, and tax and rent delinquencies. Post-World War II experience in federally aided rehabilitation and conservation suggests, furthermore, that Ihlder hopelessly underestimated the degree of technical skill and financial resources required for large-scale rehabilitation programs.

A strategy of mass housing betterment through code enforcement and rehabilitation was of dubious value also because it depended upon the cooperation and initiative of municipal bureaucracies. Ihlder soon discovered that the Bureau of Sanitation exhibited an "unusual facility for adjusting itself to a routine." It was most cooperative, to be sure, in agreeing to procedures and forms, but otherwise interpreted the Association's "considerate silence regarding long standing violations as part of the routine."[29] The Bureau of Building Inspection proved equally

[27] "Executive Director's Report, Board Meeting, December 20, 1928," Pittsburgh Housing Association, Minutes.
[28] Ihlder, *Better Dwellings.*
[29] Eleanor S. Webster, "Report on Inspections for September," October 14, 1930, Pittsburgh Housing Association, Minutes. The Association began listing violations with the Bureau of Sanitation in January, 1929. As of May 1, 1930, 755 unabated violations on 402 houses remained.

"Hooverville," Penn and Liberty, 11th to 17th Streets.

complacent about the demolition or repair of unsafe dwellings listed by the Pittsburgh Housing Association.[30] Enforcement became even more difficult when the Association extended operations to the County in 1930. Interborough "rivalry and jealousy" precluded joint action, and in some places, like McKees Rocks, "we have discovered almost complete unwillingness to cooperate on the part of health officials."[31]

Some board members of the Pittsburgh Housing Association had always questioned Ihlder's emphasis upon code enforcement. They asserted that the Association would merely duplicate the

[30] *Ibid.; Pittsburgh Press*, November 2, 1930. Of 161 properties filed with the Bureau of Building Inspection from July, 1929 to October, 1930, 82 had shown "no abatement whatever." The Association complained of a complete lack of cooperation on the part of the Bureau of Fire.
[31] "Report of Assistant Director. Extension of Work to Allegheny County," Board of Director's Meeting, October 14, 1930; "Report of Assistant Director. Work in Allegheny County" (1931), Pittsburgh Housing Association, Minutes.

work of municipal agencies. More important, no amount of regulatory effort would increase the housing supply, reduce rents, or eliminate such conditions as "unventilated rooms, crowded court spaces, privy-vaults, toilets in the open, lack of water supply, inadequate sewerage." The only way to solve the housing problem was to increase the "supply of wholesome modern homes to be rented or sold to families of low income." This could be done, presumably, through organization of limited-dividend companies.[32]

As the depression dragged on, the Association was forced to revise its original policy. In the 1930's high vacancy rates implied evictions and doubling-up of families rather than a housing surplus that would make code enforcement and rehabilitation feasible.[33] Tax and rent delinquencies accelerated nonmaintenance and the deterioration of the housing stock. The Pittsburgh Housing Association conceded, in 1933, that "slum areas of Pittsburgh have become worse, due in part to non-payment of rent with consequent financial distress to owners, and consequent neglect of repairs. Tax delinquencies have become more frequent, city revenues have fallen off and . . . enforcement of laws to protect the public health and safety has become increasingly lax."[34]

The futility of code enforcement in a context of spreading blight, evictions, and rent and tax delinquencies provided one stimulus to new housing policy in the 1930's. Declining property values and unemployment also stimulated the quest for a new approach to housing in the form of large-scale slum clearance and redevelopment. Thus, by 1933, the Pittsburgh Housing Association was advocating "reconstruction of slum or decadent areas" and "provision of low-cost housing." A crucial issue concerned the role of government in the slum clearance and redevel-

[32] David Goldner and G. Brown Hill to Board of Directors, September 27, 1929, Pittsburgh Housing Association, Minutes.
[33] "Evictions came in waves," the Association noted, "usually increasing just before the rental season. The highest wave came in the spring of 1932. During this year there were several small riots, so-called 'communists' organized to move back an evicted family's furniture as soon as the constables had moved it out." Pittsburgh Housing Association, *Three Year Report, 1931-1932-1933*, 19.
[34] *Ibid.*, 9.

opment process. "Instead of regulation of non-existent private enterprise," the Association observed, "public interest turned to government encouragement and financial support of house building, and this not only by the state but by the federal government." As for the City of Pittsburgh, the Association urged that it retain ownership of tax-delinquent property and redevelop the land for a "use that has economic or social value."[35]

The assumption that constructive environmental intervention was the exclusive prerogative of voluntary agencies had been challenged. The depression proved instrumental in persuading one segment of business and professional leadership in Pittsburgh that the historical allocation of functions to the public and private sectors was no longer viable; government, at least in the housing field, could no longer be limited to a negative, regulatory role. On the other hand, the Buhl Foundation, through its sponsorship of Chatham Village, attempted to prove that direct government intervention and subsidy were still unnecessary. The creation of Chatham Village was a classic expression of the reform process in Pittsburgh. Initiative for environmental change came from the business and professional leaders who constituted the management of the Foundation. The demonstration was conceived as the first step in the rationalization of the building industry; decision making, as in the auto industry, would be concentrated in a few large companies. Decisive environmental change would thus occur predominantly under voluntary auspices.

The Buhl Foundation was established in 1928.[36] Its executive director, Charles F. Lewis, had been an editorial writer for the *Pittsburgh Sun* until 1927, when he became editor of the *Pitts-*

[35] *Ibid.*, 6, 21, 11.

[36] Henry Buhl, Jr., who died in 1927, was the owner of Boggs and Buhl, a large department store on Pittsburgh's North Side. The original Board of Managers included John A. Fuhs, William S. Linderman, Arthur E. Braun, and Robert S. Frazier. Fuhs died within a short time and was replaced by A. W. Robertson. Except for Frazier, Chief Justice of the Pennsylvania Supreme Court, all the managers were prominent businessmen. Donald Lisio, "Investing in Pittsburgh's Progress: The History of the Buhl Foundation," unpublished Ph.D., University of Wisconsin, 1964, 36ff. This is the most complete account of the origins and development of the Foundation.

burgh Record.[37] Lewis was an ideal choice to head a foundation which, according to its benefactor, Henry Buhl, Jr., should concentrate upon the Pittsburgh area. Lewis's pride in the city exceeded mere civic boosterism; he seemed at times to view life in Pittsburgh as akin to a romp in the Elysian fields. Pittsburgh marched on the "highroad to a more certainly sustained period of happiness than it has ever known." Education and culture flourished. Civic spirit abounded as "in the press, on the platform, and from every vantage point of leadership we are summoned to have faith in Pittsburgh and to understand its place and destiny." In this atmosphere of good cheer, Lewis intimated, "wholesome criticism is becoming almost safe and may soon become respectable."[38] Social and economic problems persisted, but they could be resolved through social research and the kind of enlightened capitalism exemplified in Chatham Village.[39]

During its first year, the Buhl Foundation awarded grants in economic and social research, education, and recreation.[40] Lewis launched his explorations into housing as a possible area of investment in 1929. Through published material, interviews, and field investigations, he examined the leading experiments in nonspeculative, limited-dividend housing: the City Housing Corporation communities of Sunnyside, Long Island, and Radburn, New Jersey; the Rockefeller apartments in New York City; the Clothing Workers' apartments built in New York under the auspices of the state limited-dividend housing law of 1926; and the Julius Rosenwald Fund's Michigan Boulevard apartments in

[37] Lewis owed his appointment to Arthur Braun, banker and publisher-owner of the *Pittsburgh Sun* until 1927 (*Ibid.*, 44).
[38] Charles F. Lewis, "Pittsburgh Hails a New Day," *Pittsburgh Record*, 3 (October 1928), 3, 8; Charles F. Lewis, "The Giant Lifts His Eyes," *Pittsburgh Record*, 3 (April 1929), 5, 10.
[39] On the subject of social research, the Foundation stressed that the "search for and analysis of facts increasingly is seen to be the first essential for intelligent formulation of constructive social programs. The need for facts upon which to base social action in Pittsburgh is especially acute." Buhl Foundation, *Report for the year 1928–1929*, 34.
[40] Beneficiaries of the research grants included the University of Pittsburgh, which established a Bureau of Business Research, and the Federation of Social Agencies, which established a Bureau of Social Research.

Chicago.[41] Lewis concluded, in his report to the board of managers in the spring of 1930, that Foundation investment in housing would be economically feasible. The limited-dividend companies demonstrated that income groups avoided by commercial builders could be housed at a profit. It had been possible, even in Manhattan, to provide "high-grade housing" for less than $12.50 per room per month.[42]

Lewis also stressed the social advantages inherent in better housing. In Pittsburgh as elsewhere, slums became the "chief breeding places of ill health, poverty, ignorance, illiteracy, crime, and vice." Limited-dividend housing had led to significant behavioral and social changes. Tenants were willing to surrender "many of the uncouth liberties they enjoyed in their old environments and substitute a reign of order and convention for what had been social anarchy." The alternative to housing betterment through enlightened capitalism, Lewis warned, would be "State intervention, with all the evils attendant upon that type of paternalism."[43]

On the basis of his report, the Board of Managers authorized Lewis to explore the possibility of limited-dividend housing in Pittsburgh.[44] Chatham Village evolved directly out of the series of economic and design studies that Lewis undertook or spon-

[41] These are described in Lubove, *Community Planning in the 1920's* (cited in footnote 17).

[42] Charles F. Lewis, "Limited Dividend Housing: To the Board of Managers, June 5, 1930," *passim* (manuscript, Buhl Foundation archives). Lewis visited Sunnyside, Radburn, and the Dunbar and Amalgamated apartments. The most important conferences were those with Alexander Bing, Herbert Emmerich, Clarence Stein, and Henry Wright. Bing was president of the City Housing Corporation; its Sunnyside and Radburn communities were designed by Stein and Wright. Emmerich was vice-president of the City Housing Corporation. Others interviewed by Lewis included Charles O. Heydt, director of the Rockefeller housing enterprises; Roscoe C. Bruce, director of the Dunbar apartments; George Gove, secretary of the New York State Board of Housing; Harold S. Buttenheim, editor of *The American City*; Edwin S. Embree, president of the Rosenwald Foundation; Shelby M. Harrison, Russell Sage Foundation; and Edmund E. Day, Rockefeller Foundation.

[43] *Ibid.*, Foreward, 18, 19.

[44] The Buhl Foundation, "Pittsburgh Housing Inquiry, October 6, 1930," 2 (manuscript, Buhl Foundation archives).

sored between the spring of 1930 and the winter of 1931. These convinced the managers that a limited dividend project represented a safe investment of the capital funds of the Foundation —one that combined modest but assured profits, and unlimited social dividends.

Lewis's exhaustive investigations were organized around a series of premises. Any project would be controlled by the Buhl Foundation. It would be sufficiently large in scale to benefit from mass production techniques and progressive site-planning. The initial development over a two-year period would accommodate no less than 100 families. A commercial, not a philanthropic venture, it would be "administered strictly from the standpoint of conserving the investment and assuring a definite profit."[45] The housing would be adapted to clerical and skilled manual workers in the $2000–2500 income range, would be offered for sale, and would cost $6500–9000.[46]

Lewis realized that the managers would never risk the capital funds of the Foundation unless he demonstrated, conclusively, that "one hundred homes of the general quality, types, and price . . . could be marketed profitably in Pittsburgh in the proposed period of two years."[47] Equally important, the whole purpose of the experiment was to prove that capitalism could supply good low-cost housing at a profit. Lewis thus compiled a detailed demographic and market analysis that showed that the proposed 100 homes represented little more than 7 per cent of the average annual production of single homes in Pittsburgh between 1920 and 1929 (1337 units). Most of this housing, furthermore, was in the projected $6500–9000 price range. Leading Pittsburgh realtors, including L. W. Monteverde, F. F. Nicola, and J. W. Cree, agreed that the city was "not overbuilt in the price group under consideration."[48] Herbert Emmerich, of the City Housing Corporation of New York, corroborated their opinion.[49]

[45] *Ibid.*, 3, 4.
[46] The Foundation also hoped to provide a liberal financing plan that would keep total payments, including taxes, at $50 to $70 a month.
[47] Buhl Foundation, "Pittsburgh Housing Inquiry," 5.
[48] *Ibid.*, 13, 21, 34.
[49] Herbert Emmerich, "Report on Pittsburgh Housing Situation, November 17, 1930," 3, 4 (manuscript, Buhl Foundation archives).

Having established the economic feasibility of a limited-dividend project, Lewis stressed that it would benefit greatly from the economies of scale. These included efficient site planning and construction savings through standardization of house plans, division of labor, and discount material purchasing. The Foundation, therefore, could provide better homes and more environmental amenities at less cost than the ordinary speculative builder.[50]

Lewis originally assumed that the demonstration would consist of detached, single-family homes. There was no alternative if the dwellings were to be offered on a sales basis. Lewis's consultants unanimously agreed that preference for the detached house was too strong in Pittsburgh to overcome; "it is such a house that the average Pittsburgher looks at almost exclusively when he sets about to buy a home."[51] Lewis discovered, however, that such homes could not be provided at the contemplated price range for persons in the $2000–2500 income range. In other words, not even clerical and skilled workers could be supplied with new housing on a commercial basis—despite the resources of the Buhl Foundation, its willingness to operate on a limited-dividend investment basis, and the economies of scale.

Emmerich advised Lewis to gear the demonstration to the $2500–3600 income range. Experience at Radburn suggested that this element of the population would better appreciate the advantages of a well-planned community. Their demand for the housing, and their superior financial status, would provide an important margin of safety for the first experiment of a new housing company.[52] Planning consultants Clarence Stein and Henry Wright then estimated that detached housing on the proposed site would have to be priced at $9500–12,000, but added that costs could be greatly reduced and the overall design improved if the free-standing house was dropped in favor of the row. This would "give not only more and cheaper houses but better looking houses and would permit the grouping of garages."[53] One preliminary study prepared by Stein and Wright

[50] Buhl Foundation, "Pittsburgh Housing Inquiry," 39.
[51] *Ibid.,* 46.
[52] Emmerich, "Report on Pittsburgh Housing Situation," 6.
[53] The Buhl Foundation, "Preliminary Report of Clarence S. Stein and Henry Wright, December 29, 1930," n.p. (manuscript, Buhl Foundation

would have enabled the Foundation to construct 80 detached homes priced at an average of $10,500; a second study demonstrated that 128 row houses could be constructed on the same site and sold for $7860 to $9042.[54] The calculations of Stein and Wright led to the substitution of row for detached housing in Chatham Village. In light of local market preferences this decision led, in turn, to the substitution of rental for sales housing.

Lewis's investigations in 1930 included a search for possible sites. Any project would have to be located within city limits in order to minimize the Foundation's risk. The decision to accommodate white collar and professional persons narrowed the alternatives to a site accessible from the downtown business district. Three tracts were seriously considered, the most promising being the 45-acre Bigham estate in the Mt. Washington area of the 19th ward. An architectural study by Frederick Bigger in the fall of 1930 greatly influenced the final decision. His calculations suggested that it would be economically feasible to develop the hilly property, bounded by Virginia Avenue, Woodruff Street, Saw Mill Run Boulevard, and Olympia Park.[55]

The 19th ward was the second largest in size, but the first in population. Only one other ward had exceeded its growth rate during the 1920's, and it was in the path of population migration toward the suburban South Hills. The Mt. Washington site had other advantages. It was large enough for an experiment in neighborhood planning, close to downtown, and comparatively free of smoke. Not least important, the Bigham estate was surrounded by a "substantial, conservative, middle-class community."[56] Lewis's final report to the Board of Managers in April,

archives). See also The Buhl Foundation, "Final Report of Housing Development on the Bigham Property, April 7, 1931, by Clarence S. Stein and Henry Wright" (Buhl Foundation archives).

[54] Clarence S. Stein, *Toward New Towns for America* (Liverpool: University Press of Liverpool, 1951), 71.

[55] The Buhl Foundation, "Report of Frederick Bigger, April 17, 1931" (manuscript, Buhl Foundation archives). Along with the Bigger, Stein, and Wright studies of the Bigham property, an engineering report was prepared by the W. T. Grange Construction Company, and a boundary survey by the McBride Engineering Company.

[56] Buhl Foundation, "Pittsburgh Housing Inquiry," 69. Also, Rose C. Weibel, "Social and Housing Conditions in the Bigham District, Mt. Wash-

1931 urged that the Foundation exercise its option to acquire the property.[57]

Construction of Chatham Village began in the spring of 1931, and the first 129 dwelling units were completed within a year. A second section of 68 homes was built in 1935–1936. Grouped in rows of two to eight, the 197 Georgian-style houses contained two floors and a basement. Most garages were set off in compounds. By economic criteria, Chatham Village was a resounding success. Occupied by white collar workers, junior executives, professionals, and teachers, it experienced an extraordinarily low tenant turnover and vacancy rate. The Buhl Foundation, which invested approximately $1,600,000, received a "stable annual return in excess of 4 percent after depreciation."[58]

Chatham Village, however, did not win international acclaim because the Buhl Foundation made a profit, important as this

ington, April 21, 1931" (manuscript, Buhl Foundation archives). The population was mostly of German and Irish ancestry.

To insure that the projected housing demonstration was adapted to the needs of downtown white collar workers, the Buhl Foundation also sponsored an investigation of their housing preferences. See Theodore A. Veenstra, *Housing Status of Salaried Workers Employed in Pittsburgh* (Pittsburgh: University of Pittsburgh, Bureau of Business Research, 1932). The investigation was conducted in the spring of 1931.

[57] The Buhl Foundation, "Housing. Final Report on Housing Studies by the Director to the Board of Managers of the Buhl Foundation, April 21, 1931" (manuscript, Buhl Foundation archives), 13. The other sites that had been considered were located on the North Side and Hazelwood (15th ward). The North Side property, on Marshall Avenue near Brighton Road, was both too small and too smoky. The Hazelwood site, in the vicinity of Winterburn and Bigelow Streets, was also smoky and handicapped by its distance from the downtown business district. The Buhl Foundation, "Pittsburgh Housing Inquiry," 61–62.

[58] The Buhl Foundation, *Report for the Period Ended June 30, 1955*, 104. The only residential expansion of Chatham Village occurred in 1955–1956 when Chatham Manor, a nineteen unit, three-story elevator apartment house, was constructed. The apartments contained bedroom, living room, kitchen, and bath.

Negotiations were launched in 1959 that transformed Chatham Village into a cooperative in 1960. This was one of the first cooperatives organized under the amendment to the National Housing Act in 1959 which permitted conversion of existing rental housing with FHA insurance up to 97 percent of the value of the property. See *Pittsburgh Post-Gazette*, December 31, 1959; *Pittsburgh Press*, June 8, 1960.

was to Lewis and the Board of Managers. The economics of the demonstration interested few in comparison to the site-planning and design features (particularly since it did not, in the end, accommodate a low-income population). Wright and Stein had already experimented with most of the planning techniques at Sunnyside and Radburn: superblock subdivision; separation of pedestrian and vehicular traffic; houses fronting on park-like inner courts; generous provision for recreation and leisure (the houses occupied only 16 of the 45 acres, another 25 consisted of woods and pedestrian trails, and 4 were used for playgrounds). What made Chatham Village distinctive was the adaptation of these techniques to the hilly terrain of Mt. Washington. Wright, the principal planner, skillfully designed the row house clusters so as to minimize construction costs while exploiting the visual potentialities of the undulating site. The landscaping, by Griswold and Kohankie of Pittsburgh, softened the effect of the repetitive, brick row houses.[59]

Charles Lewis's initiative and imagination led the Buhl Foundation to invest in a housing demonstration. His receptivity to the community planning principles of Wright and Stein insured that it would become something more significant than another large residential subdivision. In the final analysis, however, the economic implications of Chatham Village were more important to Lewis than the design innovations. His major objective throughout had been to prove that capitalism could resolve the national housing problem. "Commercial practicability, within the limits of the return set," he maintained, "is regarded as the very essence of the program." Like other limited-dividend sponsors, the Buhl Foundation had insisted upon "rigid, businesslike standards," and had eschewed any "taint of philanthropy or charity." Chatham Village demonstrated, in short, the feasibility of a limited-dividend, investment approach to "community building projects."[60]

Commercial success was closely related to the scale of opera-

[59] The architects for Chatham Village were Ingham and Boyd of Pittsburgh.
[60] Charles F. Lewis, "A Moderate Rental Housing Project in Pittsburgh," *Architectural Record*, 70 (October 1931), 217; Charles F. Lewis, "Housing —The Orphan on the Doorstep," *Pittsburgh Record*, 6 (October-November 1931), 23.

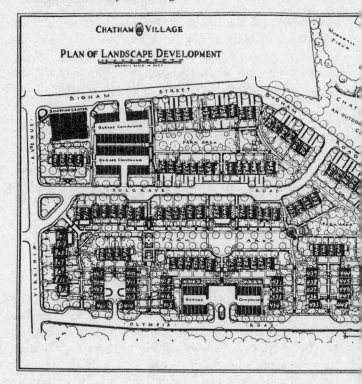

tion. This enabled the developer to reduce costs and provide a superior living environment. "At every step, from plan to marketing and administration," Lewis observed, "a limited dividend company is able to capitalize the advantages of superior intelligence and skill."[61]

It followed that solution of the national housing problem depended upon transformation of the building industry into vertically organized, mass production units, which operated on an investment basis and built entire neighborhoods rather than scattered dwelling units. The new housing industry would "look upon the nation as its field. . . . It will build large residential communities, complete entities within themselves, with schools and recreational facilities." Lewis spoke in terms of the Fords and General Motors of housing who would put "good housing

[61] Buhl Foundation, "Pittsburgh Housing Inquiry," 39.

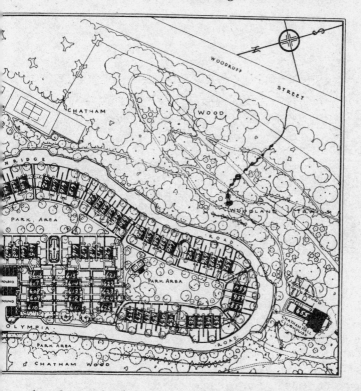

within the reach of the multitudes."[62] Capitalism had not failed in the critical area of housing and neighborhood development; it had never been tried in the sense of "completely integrated, nationally operating, home building companies, capable of applying to large-scale construction sound organization procedures and management policies."[63]

Chatham Village thus demonstrated, to Lewis's satisfaction, the commercial feasibility of limited-dividend investment housing, the economic and design advantages of large-scale development, and the need to apply "capitalistic abilities and methods" to housing and neighborhood planning.[64] It also demonstrated the need for large-scale professional management in rental hous-

[62] Lewis, "Housing—The Orphan on the Doorstep," 24.
[63] Charles F. Lewis, "An Investment Approach to Housing," American Academy of Political and Social Science, *Annals,* **190** (March 1937), 22.
[64] *Ibid.,* 20.

Chatham Village.

ing. Lewis devoted considerable attention to this issue once the decision had been made to rent rather than sell. "Management of a character equal to the physical soundness of the plant," he reported, "more than any other factor, will now determine to what degree the Foundation's investment will be secured, its income protected." Beyond this, the Foundation should exploit the opportunity "for a demonstration in management quite as unique and useful as the demonstration in community planning and house design."[65] Widespread depression foreclosures had exposed the unsoundness of the American mania for homeownership. Countless families had assumed an economic burden they could not afford. Many would not have acquired speculative, jerry-built homes, frequently financed through expensive second mortgages, if they had had a real alternative like rental housing "based upon constructive investment motives, and property management of a professional stature." At present, "absentee or amateur" landlordism prevailed.[66]

Two managerial policies dominated at Chatham Village. The

[65] The Buhl Foundation, "Housing. A Program for Administration, November 18, 1931," 3 (manuscript, Buhl Foundation archives).
[66] Charles F. Lewis, "Economic Realism in Housing," *Greater Pittsburgh*, **18** (February 1938), 8.

first was meticulous maintenance of the buildings and grounds; the second was careful tenant selection to protect the homogeneity of the community. The experimental features of Chatham Village were strictly limited to economics and planning.[67] The Buhl Foundation stressed that no tenant need "be concerned lest a socially undesirable family move next door, because a careful, but sensible, scrutiny of applicants for homes assures to every Villager good neighbors."[68] And no applicant, Lewis stressed, "should ever be permitted to know what are the bases of selection."[69] The Buhl Foundation, apparently, conceived of Chatham Village, as a sanctuary for "sound, middle class, white-collar folks who had achieved financial stability and who now wanted the social stability of just such a neighborhood of homes for their youngsters and themselves."[70]

As was suggested earlier, the resources of the Buhl Foundation, its limited-dividend, investment approach to housing, and the economies of scale added up to 197 homes "designed for white collar people with good taste."[71] Lewis, nonetheless, insisted that Chatham Village represented a viable alternative to government subsidy. It would serve its most useful purpose if it encouraged Americans to "think of housing in terms of a philosophy that is not socialistic but frankly capitalistic—a centralized, mechanized building industry that operated on an investment and neighborhood building basis.[72] Local government could assist through slum-clearance projects. Low-income groups would benefit by moving into the homes vacated by the middle

[67] Lewis stressed the importance of avoiding any impression that upper-income limitations were imposed at Chatham Village. If this happened, "upstanding, self-respecting tenants would be frightened away. The kind of people who make good tenants would not be attracted by a policy that put an income tag upon residence in The Buhl Foundation's project." Buhl Foundation, "Housing. A Program for Administration," 6.

[68] The Buhl Foundation, *A Review by the Director for the Five Years Ended June 30, 1933*, 35.

[69] Buhl Foundation, "Housing. A Program for Administration," 9.

[70] *Chatham Village News*, 14 (June 11, 1945), 1. Also, Buhl Foundation, *Chatham Village. A Modern Community of Garden Homes Combining Architectural Charm with Security and Cultured Living* (January 1932).

[71] C. V. Starrett, "Housing That Pays," *Survey Graphic*, 27 (January 1938), 24.

[72] Lewis, "An Investment Approach to Housing," 20 (cited in footnote 63).

class.[73] To substitute government subsidy for neighborhood building under private auspices would be self-defeating. It would only discourage private capital and delay the reorganization of the building industry. Political pressure would mount "rapidly, irresistibly, and ruinously," forcing government to provide "new homes—by subsidy—for ever higher and higher income groups."[74]

Lewis's formulation of the housing issue provided no clues to action in the event that capitalism failed to respond to the challenge. The building industry, in fact, remained speculative and localized. Large-scale, investment housing companies did not materialize and plant Chatham Villages throughout the land (or even in Pittsburgh). Low-income families did not move into the commodious homes vacated by the middle-class. A brilliant experiment in residential site-planning and design, Chatham Village otherwise demonstrated the bankruptcy of voluntarism as a strategy for mass housing betterment. While Lewis opposed government action in favor of a nebulous managerial revolution in the building industry, the problem of housing low-income families during a depression persisted. Indeed, squatter colonies housed almost as many persons in Pittsburgh as Chatham Village before 1936.[75] An economist estimated that elimination of the worst housing and overcrowding would require at least 27,000 dwelling units, or the total number built in Pittsburgh between

[73] Charles F. Lewis, "Let Private Capital Build Houses," *Nation's Business*, 26 (July 1938), 69.

[74] Lewis, "An Investment Approach to Housing," 19. Also, Charles F. Lewis, "The Handwriting on Slum Walls," *Pittsburgh Record* (March 1934), 9; Charles F. Lewis, "The National Housing Movement," *Greater Pittsburgh*, 15 (February 1935), 5, 21; Charles F. Lewis, "Some Economic Implications of Modern Housing," *American Economic Review*, 27 (March 1937), Supplement, 190, 194, 195.

[75] "Shantytown" alone, a colony in The Strip district composed of 90 shacks, housed 200 men in 1933. The Banksville Dump Colony and Monument Hill Colony (Tobin Street on the North Side) contained 100 and 60 men, respectively. Cellartown (29th Street on the Allegheny) originated when 30 men occupied the cellars of a demolished mill. Alpine Village (South Side) consisted of 40 cabins and 60 men. Allegheny River Colony (Highland Park Bridge area), and Monongahela Colony (south bank below Glenwood Bridge), contained 10 and 30 men, respectively. Pittsburgh Housing Association, *Housing in Pittsburgh, Three Year Report, 1931–1932–1933*, 24–27.

World War I and 1934. The depression, furthermore, exaggerated but did not cause the problem of low-income housing: "the long and short of it is that a large group of people cannot pay for even shabby housing—and a very considerable part of these could not pay for it in 1929."[76]

This observation applied with special force to the Negro population of Allegheny County, whose rate of growth exceeded that of the County as a whole for each decade from 1910 to 1940.[77]

[76] J. W. Watson, "Federal Aid in Housing," *Pittsburgh Business Review,* 5 (August 29, 1935), 2, 3. The Real Property Inventory of Allegheny County, a relief project conducted in the winter of 1934, enumerated approximately 226,000 residential dwelling structures (exclusive of hotels, clubs, dormitories, and rooming houses). Of these, about 189,000 were reported to be in good condition or needing only minor repairs; 30,000 needed major structural improvements and another 6500 were declared as unfit for habitation. The buildings contained approximately 310,000 dwelling units; of these some 45,000 were in structures requiring major improvements, and another 10,000 in structures classified as unfit for use. The larger proportion of these "bad order" dwelling units were in rental properties. J. P. Watson, "Condition of Dwelling Houses in Allegheny County," *Pittsburgh Business Review,* 5 (April 1935), 18, 26, 27.

For additional information on the Real Property Inventory and housing conditions generally in Pittsburgh during the 1930's, see University of Pittsburgh, Bureau of Business Research, *Real Property Inventory of Allegheny County* (Pittsburgh, 1937); Evelyn Riethmiller, "Rents in the Slums of Pittsburgh," *Federator,* 12 (January 1937), 11–14; James McIntyre and Evelyn Riethmiller, "Rents in the Slum Districts of Pittsburgh," *Federator,* 12 (November 1937), 234–240; Adelaide Hunter and James McIntyre, "A Study of 104 Relief Families Ejected in 1935 by Demolition of Their Homes," *Federator,* 13 (January 1938), 7–11; Edward B. Olds, "The Blighted and Prosperous Areas of Pittsburgh," *Federator,* 14 (March 1939), 59–71; Edward B. Olds, "Residential Building and Demolition as Indicators of Population Trends and Neighborhood Conditions in Pittsburgh," *Federator,* 15 (January 1940), 13–20. Useful for information on social as well as housing conditions are the *Reports* of the Pittsburgh Housing Association, and the following area studies: Albert J. Kennedy, *Social Conditions in the Twenty-Seventh Ward. A Report to the Buhl Foundation Upon a Study Made between November, 1929, and November, 1930* (December 1930); Emma Schauer, "South Side," *Federator,* 12 (September 1937), 182–189; Jane Holmes and Emma Schauer, "Brighton Woods," *Federator,* 12 (May 1937); Adelaide Hunter McCabe, "The Strip: A District in Transition," *Federator,* 15 (December 1940), 347–350.

[77] Bertram J. Black and Aubrey Mallach, *Population Trends in Allegheny County,* 4. The increase in the population of Allegheny County between

Cliff dwellers, 1930.

By 1940 the 90,060 Negroes constituted 6.4 percent of the County population. Most of them lived in Pittsburgh, where they totalled to 9.3 percent of the population.[78] As in other Northern cities, the increase in the Negro population was associated with a process of ghetto concentration. By the first decade of the twentieth century, Pittsburgh Negroes began to cluster in the 3rd and 5th wards (the Hill District), and in the 12th and 13th (East Liberty and Homewood-Brushton). Negroes, in 1940, comprised 51.14 percent of the population of the 3rd ward, 70.13 percent of the 5th, 19.43 percent of the 12th, and 16.63 percent of the 13th.[79] The Hill was Pittsburgh's Harlem; in this ghetto "ramshackle shanties, raw-faced tenements and dank cellars" lined narrow, twisting streets, labyrinth alleys, and obscure courts. Here lived "7.5 percent of Pittsburgh's population—a segment that accounts

1910 and 1940, expressed in percentages by respective decade, was 16.4, 15.9, and 2.7; the comparable growth rate for the Negro population was 56.4, 55.7, and 8.1. The Negro population of the County totalled 27,753 in 1900, 34,217 in 1910, 53,517 in 1920, 83,326 in 1930, and 90,060 in 1940.
[78] *Ibid.*, 14, 15.
[79] Pittsburgh Civic Unity Council, *Report on Population Movements and Housing Trends* (prepared for the Civic Unity Council by Bryn J. Hovde) (Pittsburgh, 1950), 10.

for 34% of the city's tuberculosis cases, 13.4% of its crime, 24.4% of all juvenile delinquency, 38.5% of all murders."[80]

If public housing was a response to the chronic shortage of low-cost housing, the decline of property values in the 1930's that enhanced the attractiveness of large-scale slum clearance, and the depression unemployment, it was also the outcome of the growth and concentration of the Negro urban population.[81] The Negro, most of all, could not be accommodated through the unsubsidized market mechanism—whether speculative or limited-dividend—because of the combination of discrimination and poverty.

The Housing Authority of Pittsburgh, established in 1937, built eight projects by 1944. Four were located in the Soho-Upper Hill-Oakland area. Two were "671" projects: Allegheny Dwellings (lower North Side) and Arlington Heights (South Side). Glen Hazel Heights and Broadhead Manor (West End) were war housing communities owned by the federal government and managed on lease by the local authority.[82] From the beginning, pub-

---

[80] "Slums and Housing," *Bulletin Index,* **110** (April 8, 1937), 8. Studies of Negro living conditions in Pittsburgh include: Abraham Epstein, *The Negro Migrant in Pittsburgh* (University of Pittsburgh, School of Economics, 1918); Wiley A. Hall, "Negro Housing and Rents in the Hill District of Pittsburgh," unpublished M.A., University of Pittsburgh, 1929; *The Social Conditions of the Negro in the Hill District of Pittsburgh* (published by the General Committee of the Hill Survey, 1930, survey conducted under the direction of Ira De A. Reid); Joseph H. Bunzel, *Negro Housing Needs in Pittsburgh and Allegheny County* (Pittsburgh Housing Association, September 1946).

[81] The most prominent advocate of public housing in Pittsburgh was George E. Evans, a Single-Taxer and realtor, who served as head of the Pittsburgh Bureau of Building Inspection under Mayor McNair, and became a city councilman in 1935. "Slums and Housing," *Bulletin Index,* **110** (April 8, 1937), 8–9; M. Nelson McGeary, *The Pittsburgh Housing Authority,* Pennsylvania State College Studies No. 14 (State College, Pa., 1943), 6–8. Important also were the contributions of the Pittsburgh Housing Association. Its executive director, Joseph P. Tufts, was active in efforts in 1935 to acquire PWA housing for Pittsburgh; in 1937 the Association helped prepare the legislation that set up a State Housing Board, and authorized the establishment of local housing authorities. Joseph P. Tufts, "Why No Federal Housing Here?" *Greater Pittsburgh,* **16** (October 1935), 11–12; Pittsburgh Housing Association, *Housing in Pittsburgh, 1934–1937,* 7, 8.

[82] The four low-rent projects were Bedford Dwellings, Addison Terrace

lic housing served as a major resource for the Negro population. Excluding Broadhead Manor, the projects accommodated 10,343 whites and 7,717 Negroes by 1944. This represented 1.6 percent of the white population of Pittsburgh compared to 12.3 percent of the Negro.[83] The proportion of Negroes would undoubtedly have been greater if half the projects had not been reserved for war workers.[84] Although public housing was a limited response to the housing needs of the low-income population, especially the Negro, and fell into disrepute after World War II, it did provide an important precedent for constructive public intervention in the physical environment.

(Terrace Village I), Wadsworth Terrace (Terrace Village IIa), and Allequippa Terrace (Terrace Village IIb). The Housing authority later classified Allequippa and Wadsworth Terraces as a single project, reducing the number to seven until the 1950's.

The "671" projects were those converted to war use; the federal government advanced a 100 percent loan for "duration plus six months."

In the 1950's the Housing Authority built a 460-unit extension to Bedford Dwellings, and the 1089-unit St. Clair Village in the South Side.

The work of the Housing Authority of Pittsburgh is described in Pittsburgh Housing Association, *Citizens Look at Public Housing: A Symposium.* . . . (1944); *The First Seven Years: A Report of the Housing Authority of the City of Pittsburgh for the Years 1937–1944;* Housing Authority of the City of Pittsburgh, *A Report to the People: Public Housing in Pittsburgh, 1938–1953.*

[83] *The First Seven Years,* 24. Broadhead Manor included 448 dwelling units for a total of 5462.

[84] The population of the war housing communities (Allegheny Dwellings, Arlington Heights, and Glen Hazel Heights) was predominantly white— 80.1 percent, 74.2 percent, and 77 percent, respectively. Negroes, on the other hand, constituted 91.9 percent of Bedford Dwellings, 50.6 percent of Addison Terrace, 43.9 percent of Allequippa Terrace, and 58.5 percent of Wadsworth Terrace. Bureau of Social Research, Federation of Social Agencies, *The Population of Public Housing,* Pittsburgh, Pa., Public Housing Reports No. 1 (June 1944).

FIVE

Planning: Form Without Substance

Planning activity in Pittsburgh during the interwar decades, like housing betterment, often hinged upon the initiative of voluntary civic and business organizations. A voluntary association, the Citizens Committee on City Plan (CCCP), even usurped the responsibility for preparing a general physical plan for Pittsburgh. Established in 1918, the CCCP became the chief vehicle through which businessmen attempted to influence the evolution of the physical environment. Its founders and officers included Charles D. Armstrong, W. L. Mellon, R. B. Mellon, James D. Hailman, and Howard Heinz. Many other prominent businessmen served on committees or provided financial support.[1]

Frederick Bigger, along with Armstrong and Hailman, had been instrumental in organizing the CCCP, and he became its chief technical adviser. Bigger hoped that a voluntary association might create awareness of the need for planning in Pittsburgh and, in the process, improve the status of the moribund City Planning Commission.[2] A native Pittsburgher, Bigger (1881–1963) received an architectural degree from the University of Pennsylvania. He practiced in Seattle and Philadelphia (1908–1913) before returning to Pittsburgh, where he became secretary

[1] Charles D. Armstrong (President of Armstrong Cork Co.) and James D. Hailman (an engineer) served as president and secretary, respectively, for many years. R. B. Mellon was vice-president; and W. L. Mellon was appointed to the Finance Committee. The Citizens Committee on City Plan of Pittsburgh was legally chartered as the Municipal Planning Association.

[2] Interview with George Baird (Executive Secretary, Pittsburgh Art Commission, 1920–1933; later Senior Research Analyst, City Planning Commission); *Progress* 6 (January 1929), 1. (*Progress* was the Newsletter of the CCCP.)

of the Municipal Art Commission, planner for the CCCP, a member of the City Planning Commission in 1922, and its chairman from 1934 to 1954. A bachelor whose life centered on his work, the "bespectacled, bald-domed" Bigger served as a liaison between public and private planning institutions, businessmen and professional planners; he "personally laid practically all the groundwork for Pittsburgh's long-range planning."[3]

Bigger was unusual in his combination of technical proficiency and social idealism. His conception of the municipal planning function was rooted in two nuclear principles. The first was the need for master or comprehensive planning. Like the businessman, Bigger aspired to a bureaucratic rationalization, or centralization of decision making as a basis for effective environmental control. This was especially imperative in Pittsburgh because of the multi-dimensional fragmentation of the community. "Having scanned the landscape carefully," Bigger explained, "one realizes that Pittsburgh is a city in which are many isolated settlements and communities, difficult or indirect of access." The foreign born exhibited the "natural tendency to live in groups according to nationality. This tendency, combined with classifications of an economic character . . . is often further intensified by the physical segregation induced by the rough topography." Superimposed upon this pattern of fragmentation was a "political system and custom which makes it possible for the inferior politician to play off one district against another." It was not surprising, therefore, that "city wide civic aspiration has been feeble."[4] It could be nurtured and expressed through a comprehensive planning mechanism.

If planning was to become anything more than a vague aspiration for community cohesion and rational control of the environment, it would be necessary to allocate greater power to professionals and government. What was the use of establishing

[3] *Bulletin Index*, 117 (July 11, 1940), 6, 7. During the 1930's, Bigger worked with the Resettlement Administration on the planning of the Greenbelt towns. He was an adviser to the Federal Housing Administration from 1940 to 1945, and in 1948 was appointed to the National Capital Planning Commission.

[4] Frederick Bigger, "Pittsburgh and the Pittsburgh Plan," *Art and Archeology*, 14 (November–December 1922), 271, 272.

public planning agencies as long as "mutual accommodation between the politician and the citizen with selfish interest limits
the exercise of technical ability?" More fundamentally, what
contribution could the planner make as long as the "important
and determining factors" in shaping the environment remained
beyond his control. Current planning practice consisted "of attempts to contrive results without having an adequate control
over causes." There would be the forms and not the substance of
planning until public power increased at the expense of private,
entrepreneurial prerogatives. A new set of legal and economic
norms had to be established, enhancing public control over land,
the distribution and density of population, and the "use and
occupancy of . . . private property."[5]

The CCCP pursued Bigger's planning objectives. Above all, it
was organized "with the single object of producing the Pittsburgh Plan, to give Pittsburgh an orderly, scientific, comprehensive program of city building." But if a master plan was
indispensable for "comfort, safety, health, convenience, utility
and beauty," it followed that the CCCP had to encourage a more
active role for public agencies in the planning process; imple-
mentation of its general plan depended upon municipal legislation and expenditure.[6] A voluntary agency could not impose a
plan upon the City of Pittsburgh.

The plan prepared by the Committee consisted of six parts.
Its first report, on "Pittsburgh Playgrounds," was published in
1920; the "Major Street Plan" followed in 1921. The remaining
documents, published in 1923, dealt with transit, parks, railroads,
and waterways. The playground and street reports, the most
influential of the six, clarify the CCCP's approach to comprehensive planning and public action.[7] The core of the playground

[5] Frederick Bigger, "Architecture and Broad Planning. III. The Limitations
of City Planning," *Journal of the American Institute of Architects*, 13 (June
1925), 200, 201, 202.
[6] The Citizens Committee on City Plan of Pittsburgh, *Pittsburgh Playgrounds. Being the First Portion of a Report Upon the Recreation System.
A Part of the Pittsburgh Plan (June, 1920)*, 3.
[7] The Transit plan dealt with street railways, focused on the central business
district, and included proposals for rapid transit. The Parks plan proposed a
city-wide system of neighborhood parks coordinated with playground and
athletic facilities. The Railroad study devoted special attention to freight

report was the development of service districts, enabling every child to reach a fully-equipped playground within a fifteen minute walk. Such a "complete and unified program of public recreation" depended, however, upon a greater degree of centralized municipal "authority and control." Ideally, the program should be administered by a single public agency.[8] The major street plan involved the "widening or otherwise increasing the traffic capacity of 108 miles of existing streets, and the creation of 22 miles of new streets."[9] The object was to develop three road systems: "metropolitan district thorofares," or roads linking the city with county highways; arteries that by-passed the central business district; and roads that provided access to undeveloped areas of the city.

The prospects for comprehensive physical planning, at least in the areas of recreation and streets, seemed promising in the early 1920's. The Pittsburgh city council officially adopted the two CCCP reports in 1922 as a "guide in the expenditure of public funds." The City Planning Commission likewise endorsed the plans "as a measuring stick for future improvements."[10] Unfortunately, while everyone agreed upon the desirability of comprehensive planning in principle, it was completely ignored in practice. The tradition of limited government was incompatible with the kind of centralized, large-scale public intervention implicit in master planning. Equally important, a conflict existed between planning and the municipal governmental structure. The CCCP stressed that it "has no political connections and no partisan purposes."[11] Its comprehensive planning objectives were presumably an expression of the public rather than any special or particularistic interest. Yet the municipal political system was designed to maximize the influence of private interest groups; the politician operated as a broker or mediator rather than the

handling improvements. The Waterways plan emphasized wharf development.

[8] Bigger, "Pittsburgh and the Pittsburgh Plan," 276; CCCP, *Pittsburgh Playgrounds*, 10.

[9] CCCP, *A Major Street Plan for Pittsburgh: A Part of the Pittsburgh Plan* (September, 1921), 9.

[10] *Progress*, 2 (December 1922), 2.

[11] *Progress*, 1 (January 1921), 5.

administrative agent of an amorphous "public interest."[12] The comprehensive planning ideals of Bigger and the CCCP were rooted in an ethos of rationalism, nonpartisanship, and the belief that political and administrative decisions could be sharply differentiated. Governmental decisions, however, were usually made on the basis of interest group pressures and coalitions, rather than commitment to a comprehensive plan that expressed the public interest.[13]

It is not surprising, in light of the incongruous values and institutional framework, that Bigger and the CCCP made little progress. Environmental change was not, to any significant degree, influenced or guided by comprehensive plans; and statutory planning agencies, as Bigger had put it, continued to contrive solutions to problems without any control over causes. The CCCP had presumed, after official adoption of its plans, that the city council would finally "follow a definite 'order of urgency' in allotting playground funds." Sections of the city with the greatest need would be served first, and younger children would receive higher priority than in the past. Youngsters below voting age, it seemed, had no influence over "those who are politically interested in recreation."[14] The CCCP discovered that its plan and promotional efforts made little difference. After years of advocating recreational planning, Bigger observed in the late 1920's that the "net result is not encouraging." City planning had stimulated "nebulous . . . public demands" more than it encouraged "technical competence."[15] The situation remained "exceedingly unpleasant" nearly 20 years after the appearance of the CCCP's recreation plan. The Bureau of Recreation and Bureau of Parks still operated independently, and no one assumed responsibility

[12] On the political function of "conflict management" and the misleading dichotomy between politics and administration, see Edward C. Banfield and James Q. Wilson, *City Politics* (Cambridge, Mass.: Harvard University Press, 1963).

[13] For an interpretation of planning as a nonpolitical function designed to express the "general interest" through preparation of a master plan, see R. G. Tugwell, "Implementing the Public Interest," *Public Administration Review*, 1 (Autumn 1940), 32–49.

[14] *Progress*, 2 (June 1922), 2, 4.

[15] Frederick Bigger, "Obstacles to the Development of a Recreation System," *American City*, 36 (June 1927), 815.

for a long-term "program of park and recreation development."[16] The City of Pittsburgh continued to acquire recreational sites, but ignored the problem of site improvement. Even with WPA assistance, not a single fully-equipped playground existed.[17]

The fate of the major street plan proved equally frustrating. "Ten years of effort," Bigger lamented, "finds us still in the early stages of the job." Streets were still regarded as "isolated units undertaken spasmodically," and "therein lies our community stupidity, for *piecemeal planning* leads us nowhere."[18] Municipal authorities, as in the case of recreation, did not hesitate to adopt plans which they then ignored. In 1924, for example, the CCCP had urged the city council to give priority to an Inter-District Traffic Circuit. This represented the portions of the Major Street Plan that bypassed the downtown area and expedited traffic between sections of the city. The council referred the proposal to the City Planning Commission which, under Bigger's direction, prepared more detailed studies and officially adopted the Inter-District Traffic Circuit in 1925.[19]

Allegheny County officials in the 1920's did not even pay lip service to the ideal of comprehensive highway planning. The CCCP was appalled when a proposed county bond issue in 1924 included an $8 million allocation for roads. The county commissioners had neither consulted the "planning bodies" nor prepared the general highway plan urged by the CCCP since 1921.[20] Among

---

[16] *Progress,* **9** (November 1937), 1, 3.

[17] "Millions have been spent in the past for the purchase of recreation sites," the CCCP complained, "but comparatively little was provided for site development. This has been true over the long 42 years since 1896 when Miss Beulah Kennard, as Chairman of the Education Department of the Civic Club, first persuaded the school authorities to permit Forbes School to be used as a summer recreation center." As far as the CCCP was concerned, not a single existing city playground was "properly equipped" for a "full recreational program." The one exception was the privately endowed Frick Park. *Progress,* **10** (October 1938), 1; *Progress,* **9** (November 1937), 7.

[18] Frederick Bigger, "Retain Antiquated Streets or Modernize?" *Progress,* **6** (October 1929), 2, 1.

[19] City Planning Commission of Pittsburgh, *Report to the City Council of Pittsburgh on the Inter-District Traffic Circuit. A Part of the Major Street Plan Proposed by the Citizens Committee on City Plan (March, 1926),* 1.

[20] *Progress,* **4** (April 1924), 1, 2; *Pittsburgh Sun,* March 19, 1924.

the planning agencies they ignored was their own County Planning Commission. Established in 1918 on an informal basis, it achieved legal status in 1923. County officials had also neglected the Joint Planning Conference, established in 1922. Composed of representatives of the CCCP, and the city and county planning commissions, it was supposed to coordinate projects affecting the two jurisdictions.[21]

The Allegheny County Planning Commission led an even more shadowy existence than its municipal counterpart. Until 1931, when it achieved independent status, it was little more than a board of review in the construction division of the County Department of Public Works. The Commission's technical staff was often usurped by the Department "without consent of the Planning Commission." Projects approved by the Commission would be revised without its knowledge. It did not propose any kind of "long-range program of public improvements" until 1936.[22]

The City Planning Commission also did little comprehensive planning. Only a minor portion of the Department's budget was devoted to the "making of the master plan," the purpose for which it had been created. The CCCP complained that the agency did not differentiate between that "very important job" and "routine and detailed planning" dealing with roads, subdivisions, or zoning.[23] The Commission, clearly, had adapted to its ambiguous mandate. By immersing themselves in routine but necessary functions, planners could apply their professional skills and avoid more sensitive, controversial issues. The path of least resistance was to concentrate on tasks that minimized conflict between the public planning function and private economic interests.

While the CCCP had developed its city plan between 1918–1923, the City Planning Commission had been occupied with the preparation of a zoning ordinance. The evolution of zoning in

[21] The CCCP was largely responsible for the formation of the Joint Planning Conference. *Pittsburgh Press*, March 17, 1924.

[22] Allegheny County Planning Commission, *Report, 1931*, 22, 25, 28; Park H. Martin, "Metropolitan Planning: Experience in Allegheny County, Pa.," *American Planning and Civic Annual* (1946), 113.

[23] *Progress*, 6 (December 1929), 6. In the first ten years of its existence, Bigger noted, the City Planning Commission "made but one analytical study of city-wide character." This involved the preparation of the zoning ordinance. *Pittsburgh Chronicle Telegraph*, March 17, 1924.

Pittsburgh illustrates why the planner might be tempted to avoid challenging major economic interests. Zoning was a conservative regulatory mechanism that was designed to protect property values. Yet it took years of hearings, compromises, and investigations before a zoning code could be enacted in the face of vociferous opposition. A concentration upon routine technical issues avoided such direct confrontation between private interests and a public agency that possessed little political leverage.

New York City enacted the nation's first comprehensive zoning code in 1916. That same year a Pittsburgh taxation study committee recommended zoning legislation in order to protect property values. "If Pittsburgh is to continue to raise practically all its revenues by taxing real estate values, steps must be taken to prevent the needless destruction of these values and to stabilize and promote their increase in every way possible."[24] The Civic Club then prepared an enabling act which failed in the 1917 session of the state legislature.[25] The CCCP, after its organization in 1918, became a leading advocate of zoning; no other single measure possessed "equal possibilities for insuring the physical, financial and social welfare of Pittsburgh's citizens."[26] The necessary enabling act was passed in 1919, and the City Planning Commission began work on an ordinance in 1920. A tentative ordinance was ready in 1921 and the final legislation, dividing the city in height, use, and area districts, was approved by the city council in 1923.

The zoning issue divided the Pittsburgh business community. Zoning was supported by the local press and those civic and business organizations—Chamber of Commerce, Civic Club, and CCCP—that possessed a community-wide, long-term perspective. They viewed zoning as a measure that would stabilize property values and, in the long run, increase them by preventing congestion and incompatible land use. Zoning was opposed by the Pitts-

[24] *Report of the Committee on Taxation Study, To Council of the City of Pittsburgh, Pennsylvania (November 13, 1916),* 20.
[25] Civic Club of Allegheny County, "Districting and Zoning: What It is and Why Pittsburgh Should do it," *Second Special Bulletin,* January 1, 1918, 8. The Civic Club prepared the enabling bill at the request of the Pittsburgh Taxation League.
[26] *Progress,* 3 (January 1923), 4.

burgh Real Estate Board, Pittsburgh Board of Trade, and the savings and loan associations—groups who viewed their interests in terms of maximizing building or real estate operations at all times and everywhere.

Much of the opposition centered upon the building height restrictions. According to the Pittsburgh Real Estate Board, they "serve no good purpose, and . . . retard the city's growth and prosperity." The Board of Trade emphasized that Pittsburgh's topography, which confined the downtown business district, made tall buildings necessary. The Board also objected, however, to the area and land use restrictions in the proposed ordinance; they presumably would "eliminate from 50 to 75 percent of house building." Similarly, T. A. Watkins, a prominent realtor, maintained that his firm had built 800 homes in recent years, not one of which would have been economically feasible under the zoning ordinance.[27]

Opponents of zoning argued that it was an abuse of the police power as well as a threat to the economic progress of the community. The spokesman for Pittsburgh's trust companies complained at a council hearing that the "authors of the ordinance have gone on from prohibiting nuisances to the adoption of a policy to impress aesthetic standards of the moment on the community." In attempting to legislate the city beautiful, they menaced "some well settled principles of individual liberty."[28]

In a study of the evolution of the pioneer New York zoning code, S. J. Makielski has emphasized the dominance of "local and special interests in zoning matters." They benefited from a "political system that linked interest groups and party politics to zoning through the Board of Estimate and the Board of Standards and Appeals."[29] Similarly, broad powers of amendment and variance delegated to the city council, Planning Commission, and Board

[27] *Pittsburgh Realtor*, June 26, 1923, 3, and July 17, 1923, 5; *Arguments Against the Proposed Zoning Ordinance for Pittsburgh, Pennsylvania Submitted to the City Council. And the Replies Thereto by the Department of Law and the Department of City Planning, July, 1923*, 41.

[28] *Ibid.*, 4. Although the Chamber of Commerce generally endorsed the ordinance, it did express some reservations about the height of buildings restrictions. *Pittsburgh Sun*, April 21, 1923.

[29] Stanislaw J. Makielski, Jr., *The Politics of Zoning: The New York Experience* (New York: Columbia University Press, 1966), 41.

of Adjustment enabled Pittsburgh property owners, realtors, and builders to exert considerable influence. Real estate interests who had opposed zoning were also appeased by the appointment of J. W. Cree, Jr., to the Board of Adjustment. Vice-president of the Pennsylvania Real Estate Association and director of the Commonwealth Trust Co., he had "fought every paragraph of the ordinance before Council" on behalf of the Pittsburgh Real Estate Board.[30] Between amendments and liberal variation rulings, "one thing became gradually more and more apparent." There persisted, according to the CCCP, "the feeling that the right of the individual property holder to market his property is superior to the right of the community to control development."[31]

The 1920's were a bleak era for those who advocated comprehensive planning and constructive public intervention in the physical environment. The city council had officially adopted the CCCP recreation and major street plans, but did not seem inclined to follow them in practice. The county commissioners had ignored all the planning agencies in the bond issue of 1924, which included major expenditures for highways. The Allegheny County Planning Commission achieved legal status in 1923, but did little planning and had virtually no power. The preparation and administration of the zoning ordinance, rather than master planning, preempted the resources of the City Planning Commission. Zoning, furthermore, was a negative, regulatory power that the Commission shared with other municipal authorities. There existed no coherent, centralized mechanism to guide the physical development of the community. Responsibility was diffused among the voluntary and statutory planning agencies that had proliferated since 1911, the political authorities, municipal bureaucracies, and private interests. Increasingly concerned with such problems as adapting the street system to the automobile, the suburban migration that the automobile facilitated, and the future of the central business district, some businessmen and planners looked to metropolitan government by the late 1920's for a solution. Since the 1910 census "Pittsburgh has gone on placidly content to let her inhabitants cluster their homes in the outlying suburbs without making any move toward educating

[30] *Pittsburgh Realtor,* September 11, 1923, 6, and January 1, 1924, 3.
[31] *Progress,* 5 (October 1928), 5.

them in the value of becoming a part of the central corporate body." The 1920 census returns were alarming. Pittsburgh, dropping behind Detroit and Cleveland, had "lost its coveted place in population among the large centers of the country."[32]

It was misleading to suggest that the City of Pittsburgh had been complacent about the suburban challenge. Despite the indignation aroused by the absorption of Allegheny in 1907, Pittsburgh continued to swallow up boroughs and townships while introducing wholesale annexation bills into the state legislature.[33] This unrelenting annexationist pressure encouraged the suburbs to adopt metropolitan government as a strategy of self-defense. The League of Boroughs and Townships of Allegheny County, under the leadership of Joseph T. Miller, assumed the initiative in seeking an alternative to annexation that would satisfy both

[32] John P. Cowan, "U. S. Census of 1920—What About Pittsburgh?," *Pittsburgh First,* 1 (July 26, 1919), 1; "Chamber Hears Appeal for Annexation of Suburban Communities," *Pittsburgh First,* 2 (July 24, 1920), 1.
[33] After the annexation of Allegheny, the City of Pittsburgh absorbed the following territories in whole or in part between 1908 and 1928.

Territory Annexed	Date of Entry	Annexed Area Acres
West Liberty Borough	1908	1,751
O'Hara Township	1908	207
Beechview Borough	1909	210
Union Township (part)	1910	58
Baldwin Township	1912	152
Ross Township (part)	1916	10
Spring Garden Borough	1920	124
Penn Township (part)	1920	1
Chartiers Township (part)	1920	11
Chartiers Township	1921	2,190
Reserve Township (part)	1922	145
St. Clair Borough	1923	622
Lower St. Clair Township (part)	1924	52
Frick Park (Swissvale)	1925	24
Carrick Borough	1926	1,202
Knoxville Borough	1927	192.75
Westwood Borough	1927	429.29
Union Township	1928	850

See *Progress,* 5 (June 1928).

Pittsburgh and suburban interests. The League had been organized in 1910–1911 in response to the "Allen Force Bill," a measure that would have forced many of the boroughs and townships to share the fate of Allegheny.[34] Another major threat to suburban autonomy appeared in 1919, when a metropolitan district bill creating a "super-government" was introduced. The League successfully resisted this measure, and a similar one in 1921. Finally, the League countered the metropolitan district legislation of 1923 with a proposal for a commission to study the issue on condition that the mayor of Pittsburgh withdraw the annexation bill.[35]

The Commission to Study Municipal Consolidation, appointed by the governor of Pennsylvania in 1923, consisted of representatives of Pittsburgh, the third-class cities, and boroughs and townships of Allegheny County. It ruled out both annexation and a metropolitan district arrangement for limited public works or improvement projects. The latter had several disadvantages. It multiplied the number of governmental units with tax or bond powers not directly responsible to the electorate, and did not provide for "coherent planning and co-ordinated effort in the solution of the closely related problems of the metropolitan area."[36] Most important, "it would make no change in the census rating of the City of Pittsburgh"; yet the "population question is of the greatest importance in the minds of the vast majority of the people affected and desiring the change."[37] Influenced by the American federal system of government, the Commission proposed a federated consolidation of city and county.[38] Communities

[34] "Borough Leader Sees Metropolitan Plan as Only Guarantee Against Forcible Annexation," Greater Pittsburgh, 9 (March 10, 1928), 7.
[35] Ibid., 7; H. Marie Dermitt, "Metropolitan Growing Pains in Allegheny County," National Municipal Review, 29 (September 1940), 580–581; Martin L. Faust, "The Pittsburgh Metropolitan Plan," University of Pittsburgh Record, 3 (October 1928), 24; "Metropolitan District Plan Halted," Pittsburgh First, 4 (April 21, 1923), 8; Rowland A. Egger, "The Proposed Charter of the Federated 'City of Pittsburgh,'" American Political Science Review, 23 (August 1929), 718.
[36] Pennsylvania, The Commission to Study Municipal Consolidation in Counties of the Second Class, Report of the Commission, February 15, 1927, 17.
[37] Ibid., 18; Pittsburgh Post, March 18, 1925.
[38] The Commission had turned directly "to a study of the original Constitu-

would retain their identity and most of their powers, while the central authority would assume existing county powers and any others enumerated in the charter.

The Commission prepared an enabling amendment to the state constitution authorizing creation of a federated City of Pittsburgh. It was approved by the legislature in 1926 and 1927, and by the state electorate in 1928.[39] During its journey through the legislature, the amendment underwent one crucial revision. The Commission's amendment required that a charter for the federated city had to receive a majority of all votes cast in Allegheny County, and a majority vote in a majority of the communities. But as the amendment emerged from the state legislature, ap-

tion of the United States." Joseph T. Miller, "We Vote on a Charter," *Pittsburgh Record*, 3 (June 1929), 6. The Commission leaned heavily upon political scientists in its research and investigations. The director of research was Thomas H. Reed, Professor of Political Science, University of Michigan, and director of the Bureau of Government. Other consultants included Paul Studensky, National Municipal League; Lent D. Upson, director, Detroit Bureau of Governmental Research, and lecturer in political science, University of Michigan; Chester E. Rightor, Detroit Bureau of Governmental Research and lecturer in municipal finance, University of Michigan; Martin L. Faust, Department of Political Science, University of Pittsburgh.

[39] In Allegheny County, the amendment was approved by a vote of 149,808 to 64,363. It was defeated only in the third class cities.

	Yes	No
Pittsburgh	81,818	21,542
Third-class cities		
Clairton	575	797
Duquesne	767	996
McKeesport	1,040	7,968
	2,382	9,761
Boroughs	49,279	21,830
Townships	16,239	11,230
Total	149,808	64,363

Rowland A. Egger, "City-County Consolidation in Allegheny County, Pennsylvania," *American Political Science Review*, 23 (February 1929), 122.

proval of a charter required a majority vote of the county, and a two-thirds majority in a majority of communities.[40]

The Commission began work on a charter after the state electorate approved the amendment in the fall of 1928. Submitted to the legislature in March, 1929, it provided for a governing body of seven commissioners and major innovations in governmental structure. The charter authorized the creation of special assessment improvement districts, consolidation of the city and county welfare departments, abolition of the minor judiciary, higher standards for volunteer fire departments, and federated responsibilities in health, water, police protection, and other areas. But "vigorous opposition from local political interests," including the judiciary and firemen's organizations, forced amendment of the charter. The consolidated welfare department was eliminated, along with provisions for judicial reform and "all reference to the departments of . . . safety, planning, parks and recreation, public art, personnel, and research." The revised charter went to the voters of Allegheny County in June, 1929. It would have passed if the Commission amendment had not been revised to require a two-thirds majority in the majority of communities. Pittsburgh would have established the first metropolitan government in the United States if not for what may have been a fluke—a "printer's option in setting his type."[41]

---

[40] According to Joseph Miller, the state senate had changed the Commission's proposal for a majority vote in a majority of communities to a majority vote in two-thirds of the communities. The house amended this to a two-thirds majority in a majority of communities, and the change was accepted by the senate. See Joseph T. Miller, "Metropolitan Plan Executive Committeemen Think Harrisburg Error Not Fatal," *Pittsburgh First*, 8 (June 12, 1926), 3.

[41] Joseph T. Miller, "The Pittsburgh Consolidation Charter," *National Municipal Review*, 18 (October 1929), 606; and Miller, "Metropolitan Plan Executive Committeemen Think Harrisburg Error Not Fatal," 3. H. Marie Dermitt of the Pittsburgh Civic Club maintained, however, that the "joker" was deliberate; it was inserted in the final hours of the 1926 legislative session by "enemies of the consolidated city plan." Dermitt, "Metropolitan Growing Pains in Allegheny County," 581. If the change was deliberate, it is not known who was responsible.

The charter required for passage a two-thirds majority in 62 of the 123 municipalities in Allegheny County. It received such a majority in 50 communities. The election returns, based on the two-thirds requirement, were as follows.

The 1920's witnessed movements for metropolitan government and comprehensive planning in Pittsburgh, which had little practical significance. The importance of the interwar decades, as far as planning and environmental intervention were concerned, derives from the concrete problems posed by the automobile and downtown. Attempts to deal with these issues eventually paved the way for large-scale renewal of the physical environment, involving a new conception of the public role.

As early as 1921, J. D. Hailman of the CCCP observed that "congestion has reached a serious point in the downtown business district." Like other cities, Pittsburgh could not cope with the "increasing traffic burden . . . due to the . . . number of passenger and trucking automobiles." The Chamber of Commerce agreed that "traffic congestion becomes a greater handicap to the business and industries of the entire metropolitan district every year." A Pittsburgh official described "traffic control" as "one of the gravest city problems."[42] Interest in road and highway develop-

	Carried	Lost
Cities	1	3
Boroughs	34	32
Townships	15	38
	50	73

The charter would have passed on the basis of the Commission requirement of a majority vote in a majority of communities, and the state senate requirement of a majority vote in two-thirds of the communities. Election returns, based on a simple majority, were as follows.

	Carried	Lost
Cities	1	3
Boroughs	52	14
Townships	29	22
	82	39

Two townships were tied.
"The Present Status of Pittsburgh Metropolitan Plan," *Greater Pittsburgh*, 10 (October 12, 1929), 75.

[42] James D. Hailman, "A Major Street Plan for Pittsburgh," Thirteenth Annual Conference on City Planning, *Proceedings (1921)*, 128, 132; "Pittsburgh's Needed Street Changes," *Pittsburgh First*, 6 (July 19, 1924), 9;

The Auto Era: Boulevard of the Allies, 1937.

ment among business groups and planners reached a climax in 1939 when the CCCP (renamed the Pittsburgh Regional Plan-

Charles B. Prichard, "Legal Aspects of Traffic Control," Thirteenth Annual Conference on City Planning, *Proceedings (1921)*, 138.

ning Association) employed Robert Moses to prepare an "Arterial Plan for Pittsburgh." The Moses report, furthermore, reveals the extent to which highway improvement schemes by the late 1930's were linked to revitalization of the central business district—Pittsburgh's Golden Triangle. "We were asked," Moses explained, "to investigate the arterial problem of Pittsburgh with particular reference to the improvement of conditions in the Triangle. The basic assumption of the sponsors of this report was that the Triangle was to be preserved and made attractive by means of arterial, park, and other improvements."[43] In its emphasis upon the problems of downtown and specific recommendations, the Moses plan provides an important link between the interwar era and the Pittsburgh "Renaissance."

Moses recognized that a key to renewal of the Triangle was elimination of the railroad facilities that blighted the Point. The Wabash property was "dead" and the B & O station and tracks were "moribund." The major problem was the Pennsylvania Railroad, occupying a "grossly disproportionate amount of land" and constituting a "major cause of traffic difficulties, uneven and haphazard development and civic ugliness."[44] Traffic control and redevelopment hinged also upon elimination of the trolleys, a solution to the vexing problem of automobile parking and, most important, a series of arterial improvements to link downtown to other districts but allow through traffic to bypass the area. The major projects recommended by Moses included a Duquesne Way along the Allegheny River connecting the Manchester Bridge to the Eleventh Street Pennsylvania Bridge; a crosstown boulevard linking Duquesne Way, Bigelow Boulevard, Liberty Bridge, and Boulevard of the Allies; and a parkway east to Wilkinsburg along the Monongahela. Finally, Moses proposed the creation of a park at the Point.[45]

[43] Robert Moses, *Arterial Plan for Pittsburgh. Prepared for the Pittsburgh Regional Planning Association, November, 1939*, 3.
[44] *Ibid.*, 7.
[45] Along with Point Park, Duquesne Way, the Crosstown Boulevard and the Parkway East, Moses recommended five other projects.

   Wabash Crossing and Plaza. (This involved the conversion of the Wabash tunnel and bridge into a highway route from the South Hills across the Monongahela into the Triangle. An important object was to relieve the traffic pressure on the Liberty Tunnel and Bridge, and other bridges over the Monongahela.)

The Moses plan ignited a furious controversy which, oddly enough, revealed the consensus in Pittsburgh by 1939 on the need for downtown renewal and most of the specific projects recommended. The controversy centered on who deserved credit for the proposals. Park Martin, county planning engineer, maintained that seven of the nine recommendations had been included in the 1936 improvement program devised by the County Planning Commission; and the Commission chairman resented the fact that businessmen had spent $50,000 "getting an outsider to bring in a report which contained nothing we had not already considered."[46] The City Planning Commission maintained that it had "been urging those same projects for some time."[47] Frederick Bigger, "ahead of his time for so long that he is slightly bitter over waiting for the world to catch up with him," was allegedly "critical of the much-touted Moses Report as a mere rewrite of what he has been saying for 20 years or more."[48] Early in 1940 the City and County Planning Commissions, Chamber of Commerce, and Pittsburgh Regional Planning Commission agreed that

2. Liberty Tunnel Grade Eliminations. (Elimination of highway grades at the south and north ends of the Liberty Tunnel.)
3. Saw Mill Run Improvement (Improvement in the alignment and right of way on the Saw Mill Run Boulevard connecting the Banksville Circle with the West End Bridge.)
4. Manhattan Street Improvement. (Widening of Manhattan Street by acquisition of a 100-foot strip on the west side of the street between the West End Bridge and Pennsylvania Railroad at California Avenue.)
5. Etna-Sharpsburg Highway Improvement. (Improvement of the state road through Sharpsburg from Highland Park Bridge to Etna on a new right of way.)

[46] *Pittsburgh Sun–Telegraph,* December 10, 1939. The County Planning Commission objected to the Manhattan Street Improvement; it preferred extension of the Ohio River Boulevard to the Triangle. A supplementary improvement favored by the Commission was a North Side bridge to bypass congestion in the Perrysville, West View, and Perrysville Avenue districts. The Commission was also indifferent to a Point Park. *Pittsburgh Post–Gazette,* December 9, 1939.

[47] *Pittsburgh Press,* December 17, 1939. The City Planning Commission dissented from two Moses recommendations. Instead of Wabash Crossing and Plaza, it proposed a new bridge and tunnel to the South Hills. And it preferred to connect Ohio River Boulevard and the West End Bridge by improving two streets rather than widening Manhattan Street.

[48] *Bulletin Index,* 117 (July 11, 1940), 7.

priority should go to the Duquesne Way, followed by the Cross-town route.[49]

The Moses report helps clarify the sources of environmental change in Pittsburgh and, specifically, the origins of the physical renewal program after World War II. First, the Moses plan was sponsored by a rejuvenated Pittsburgh Regional Planning Association. Under the leadership of its new executive director, Wallace Richards, it would serve as the technical and planning arm of the Allegheny Conference on Community Development after 1945. Second, the Moses study anticipated or publicized many of the key renewal projects: Point redevelopment; Point Park; Duquesne Way; the Penn-Lincoln Parkway; the Crosstown Boulevard; and the massive Lower Hill slum clearance. Third, the report reflected a growing concern about the future of the central business district. In 1939, the same year the Moses plan was released, a Golden Triangle Division of the Chamber of Commerce was organized. Richard K. Mellon served as chairman of the group, whose object was to "crystallize citizen effort behind a movement to stop depreciation of real estate values within the Golden Triangle by making it a better place in which to work and transact business."[50] The mood of impending crisis intensified during the War, and became a major catalyst of the "Renaissance." Fourth, a new generation of business leadership, embodied in Richard K. Mellon, realized that an unprecedented crisis situation required a new strategy of environmental intervention. The major programs—Point renewal, Point Park, highways, flood control, and smoke control—could not be implemented under voluntary auspices, no matter how powerful. The post-World War II business elite understood that attainment of private economic objectives necessitated a dramatic expansion of public powers and expenditures.

[49] Pittsburgh City Planning Commission, Minutes, January 9, 1940. It was generally agreed that completion of the Inter District Traffic Circuit took highest priority.
[50] "Reports of Chamber Divisions: Golden Triangle Division," *Greater Pittsburgh*, 21 (February 1940), 11.

SIX

The Pittsburgh Renaissance: An Experiment in Public Paternalism

In explaining the origins of Pittsburgh's massive physical renewal program following World War II, one cannot exaggerate the importance of the crisis atmosphere that pervaded the community. This led to drastic modification of the historic formula that had delegated constructive responsibility for intervention to voluntary institutions. The foundation of the entire Renaissance effort was the use of public powers and resources to preserve the economic vitality of the central business district (CBD) and, more broadly, the competitive economic position of the Pittsburgh region. In essence, the Pittsburgh Renaissance represented a response to a crisis situation, one that precipitated a dramatic expansion of public enterprise and investment to serve corporate needs; it established a reverse welfare state.

There is no doubt that Pittsburgh confronted disaster in the 1940's. Despite record wartime production and employment, the district could "boast of few important new industries, and the gain in population has been limited." Many persons "have been apprehensive—some of them definitely pessimistic—regarding the prospects for the Pittsburgh district."[1] By 1945 "large corporations which had long made their headquarters in Pittsburgh had actually taken options on properties in other cities and were laying plans to build skyscrapers there and move their offices." These included Westinghouse, Alcoa, and U. S. Steel. Corporate

[1] Bevard Nichols, "Pittsburgh Looks Ahead," *Pittsburgh Business Review*, 12 (July 30, 1942), 17. Also, Adolph O. Frey, "Working Together for Pittsburgh," *Greater Pittsburgh*, 27 (March 1946), 16–17.

managerial and technical personnel and their wives "didn't want to live and raise their families under . . . prevailing environmental conditions." A blanket of smoke choked "the city much of the time. There are floods almost every year. Hundreds of communities dump their raw sewage into Pittsburgh's rivers. . . . Housing is substandard. No major highway has been built and none is in design." Pittsburgh, in short, was "not a fit place in which to live and work and raise a family. That being the case, the responsible citizenry of the city faced a tough decision. No longer could they vacillate, rationalize, compromise. . . . Either they would stay and eventually rebuild the core of the central city, or they would get out and take their industries with them."[2]

One crucial circumstance that influenced the future of Pittsburgh was the assumption by a "whole group of younger leaders" of "positions of executive responsibility and power."[3] Their emergence and involvement in the creation of Pittsburgh's reverse welfare state was, in turn, associated with one man's decision to rebuild rather than abandon Pittsburgh. Richard King Mellon assumed control of the family enterprises in the late 1930's, following the death of his father, Richard Beaty, and uncle,

[2] Adolph W. Schmidt, *The Pittsburgh Story* (booklet, remarks at luncheon in honor of International Press Institute at University of Pittsburgh, April 19, 1958), n.p.; John J. Grove, *How Businessmen Can Lead in Improving Environment* (mimeographed address, National Community Development Forum, Chamber of Commerce of the United States, Greensburg, Pa., February 2, 1967), 3; H. J. Heinz II, *Newspaper Leadership in Community Action* (mimeographed address, 80th Convention of the American Newspaper Publishers Association, New York, April 27, 1966), 6; Edward J. Magee, *The Pittsburgh Story* (mimeographed address, Twin City Metropolitan Seminar, Minneapolis, November 10, 1966), 1–2.

For other descriptions of the postwar crisis in Pittsburgh, see "Pittsburgh Renascent," *Architectural Forum*, 91 (November 1949), 59–60; "Pittsburgh's New Powers," *Fortune*, 35 (February 1947), 69–77, 182–184, 186–187; Karl Schriftgiesser, "The Pittsburgh Story," *Atlantic Monthly*, 187 (May 1951), 66–69; "Cities: Pittsburgh Comes Out of the Smog," *Newsweek*, 34 (September 26, 1949), 25–26, 29; George Sessions Perry, "The Cities of America: Pittsburgh," *Saturday Evening Post*, 219 (August 3, 1946), 14–15, 46–48; Herbert Kubly, "Pittsburgh: The City that Quick-Changed from Unbelievable Ugliness to Shining Beauty in Less than Half a Generation," *Holiday*, 25 (March 1959), 80–87, 152–156.

[3] Heinz, *Newspaper Leadership in Community Action*, 6.

Andrew.[4] In 1946 the family interests were consolidated in T. Mellon and Sons, and new executives arrived in Pittsburgh to head the Mellon concerns: General Brehon Somervell at Koppers; George H. Love at Pittsburgh Consolidation Coal; Frank Denton at Mellon Bank; and Sidney W. Swensrud at Gulf Oil. "The blunt fact about Pittsburgh's changing scene," *Fortune* reported, "is that a new generation is in power. . . . It begins in the Mellon empire, extends through Big Steel, and runs through the other power groupings."[5]

The main vehicle through which the new corporate elite participated in the Renaissance effort was the Allegheny Conference on Community Development (ACCD). It was established in 1943 when Mellon convened a small group to discuss Pittsburgh's future.[6] From the conference evolved the idea of "forming a non-profit, non-partisan civic organization, to be devoted to research and planning, to develop an over all community improvement program."[7] Wallace Richards, director of the Pittsburgh Regional Planning Association since 1937, played a key role in establishing the ACCD. Mellon had become president of the agency in 1941, and Richards emphasized to him the need for a comprehensive postwar planning program.[8] Richards' involvement suggests that the ACCD was the product of professional as well as top corporate initiative. Dr. Robert E. Doherty, president of Carnegie Tech, and Dr. Edward Weidlein, director of Mellon Institute,

[4] The evolution of the Mellon family business empire is discussed in Charles J. V. Murphy, "The Mellons of Pittsburgh," *Fortune*, 76 (October 1967), 121–129, 238, 240, 244, 249, 250–251, 254; and "The Mellons of Pittsburgh," Part II, *Ibid.* (November 1967), 159–161, 225–226, 228, 233–234, 236; also "Mr. Mellon's Patch," *Time*, 54 (October 3, 1949), 11–14. The major Mellon enterprises include Gulf Oil, Alcoa, Koppers Co., Carborundum Co., and Mellon National Bank and Trust Company.
[5] "Pittsburgh Remodels Itself," *Business Week* (March 12, 1949), 67; "Pittsburgh's New Powers," *Fortune*, 35 (February 1947), 73. Also, "Pittsburgh Rebuilds," *Fortune*, 45 (June 1952), 90.
[6] According to Park Martin, the conference included Mellon, Alan Scaife, Dr. Edward R. Weidlein, and Wallace Richards. Park H. Martin, "Pittsburgh's Miracle is One of Leadership," (typed paper, December 1955, Allegheny Conference on Community Development, files), 3.
[7] *Ibid.*
[8] "Cities: Pittsburgh Comes Out of the Smog," *Newsweek*, 34 (September 26, 1949), 26; Schriftgiesser, "The Pittsburgh Story," 67.

were both prominent in the early planning and administration of the Conference; it became an effective force after Park H. Martin, an engineer-planner, was appointed executive director in 1945.

Civic organization in Pittsburgh was not new; Pittsburgh and other American cities were the graveyard of citizen organizations established to promote environmental or social change. What made the ACCD unique was its success, and this requires explanation. Richard Mellon's leadership and the recruitment of the corporate elite provided the ACCD with extraordinary potential power; but a policy decision adopted when the Conference was first established in 1943 insured that the power would be exercised. This was the requirement that members of the executive committee participate personally in its deliberations, and as individuals rather than representatives of any corporation.[9]

[9] The ACCD formally originated at a luncheon meeting held at the William Penn Hotel in Pittsburgh, May 24, 1943. Robert Doherty, president of Carnegie Tech, served as chairman. He spoke of the need for "resuscitation of a devitalized and deteriorating metropolitan area," adding that it "seemed to Dr. Weidlein and me and to a few others with whom we have talked that a citizens committee or conference, such as this group, might sponsor that general coordination of study and planning that appears so essential." It was then agreed that the group would constitute itself as a Citizens Sponsoring Committee on Post-War Planning for the Metropolitan Area of Allegheny County. It was decided at a second meeting, June 29, 1943, that participation in the conference and in committees "should be on an individual citizen basis." See ACCD, "Minutes of the Organization Meeting of a Citizens Conference on the Post-War Situation for Allegheny County, May 24, 1943"; "Minutes of Meeting of Allegheny County Conference on Post-War Community Planning, June 29, 1943"; ACCD, *Purpose, Organization and Progress* (June 21, 1944); ACCD, *Progress Report to Sponsors* (November 1, 1944).

The Conference originally consisted of a forty-odd member Citizens' Sponsoring Committee, and a large number of committees headed by an executive committee. The latter, in 1945, included Dr. Robert Doherty, chairman; Dr. Edward R. Weidlein, vice-chairman; Wallace Richards, secretary; J. Steele Gow; Edgar J. Kaufmann; Leslie J. Reese. "Allegheny County to Have a Check Up," *Greater Pittsburgh*, 26 (September 1945), 16–17.

For a detailed analysis of the background of the men on the executive committee in 1958–1959, see Arnold J. Auerbach, "The Pattern of Community Leadership in Urban Redevelopment: A Pittsburgh Profile," unpub-

The Conference's effectiveness was also associated with its use of technical and professional skills. The ACCD established close ties to the leading planning and research agencies of the areas, including the Pittsburgh Regional Planning Association and Pennsylvania Economy League, Western Division. Indeed, the Pittsburgh Regional served, for all practical purposes, as the technical and planning arm of the ACCD.[10] The ACCD did not simply advocate general policies; it sponsored concrete, detailed plans prepared by engineers, architects, economists, and other experts. This ability to command unlimited technical skills contrasted sharply with most civic organizations, and especially with neighborhood citizens' groups.

The policy statements and plans of the ACCD were not only preceded by extensive research, but also by consultation with the voluntary and public agencies affected by any proposal. The same strategy of consensus was used with the local press.[11] By avoiding public controversy, the ACCD could more readily identify its programs with the community interest.

The effectiveness of the ACCD depended ultimately upon the cooperation of Mayor David Lawrence and the City-County Democratic political machine. "The future," as Lawrence explained, "was to establish the working relationships between the Democratic administration and Richard Mellon." Lawrence paid particular tribute to Richards and to Mellon adviser Arthur B. Van Buskirk as the men who most "sensed the necessity of uniting public and private action for Pittsburgh's advancement." Through their efforts, in large measure, Pittsburgh pioneered "in municipal techniques which have since become commonplace."[12]

---

lished Ph.D., University of Pittsburgh, 1960. Auerbach found that a majority, 13 of the 25, were born within a 50-mile radius of Pittsburgh; 19 were graduates of Princeton, Yale, and Harvard; 13 were Presbyterian and 4 Episcopalian; all were registered Republicans. By the mid-1950's, the self-perpetuating Citizens Sponsoring Committee consisted of 100 members. It elected the Conference officers and executive committee. Allegheny Conference on Community Development, *Presents* (1956), 2.

[10] The general policy of the ACCD was to use existing organizations for research and planning wherever possible.

[11] Park H. Martin, "The Allegheny Conference—Planning in Action," American Society of Civil Engineers, *Proceedings,* 78 (May 1952), reprint, 2.

[12] David L. Lawrence (as told to John P. Robin and Stefan Lorant),

These techniques included extensive use of the "authority" mechanism in the renewal process and dependence upon the resources of every level of government. Thus the Pittsburgh civic coalition linked Democrat and Republican, businessman and politician, federal, state, and local government; and it adopted any administrative expedient that would serve its purposes.

Finally, the ACCD was successful because it forged a consensus on community policy. The ACCD could mold a powerful civic coalition because no one seriously challenged its proposition that the goal of community policy was revitalization of the CBD and ultimately the regional economy. "The need for preserving and protecting the stability of the Golden Triangle," Park Martin emphasized, "was recognized and accepted, and the program deliberately placed great emphasis on this area." Public officials agreed with the "civic leaders" that "the values of the Downtown must be preserved and strengthened before all else."[13]

The establishment of the reverse welfare state, and the prestige of the ACCD, hinged upon three projects in the early days of the Renaissance. All three—Point Park, smoke control, and flood control—had long been advocated in Pittsburgh, and they demonstrated the use of public power or investment to promote private economic ends. As Wallace Richards explained, "the

"Rebirth," in Stefan Lorant, *Pittsburgh: The Story of an American City* (Garden City: Doubleday, 1964), 402, 408, 411. Lawrence noted that Richards had been brought to Pittsburgh by Frederick Bigger, and that he "enlarged the scope of Mellon's interest in public problems, and became his civic adviser" (p. 406). Lawrence's political background and role in the civic coalition are discussed in Frank Hawkins, "Lawrence of Pittsburgh: Boss of the Mellon Patch," *Harper's Magazine*, 213 (August 1956), 55–61; Jeanne R. Lowe, "Rebuilding Cities—and Politics," *Nation*, 186 (February 8, 1958), 118–121; Sally O. Shames, "David L. Lawrence, Mayor of Pittsburgh: Development of a Political Leader," unpublished Ph.D., University of Pittsburgh, 1958. A more general account of the Renaissance appears in Lowe, *Cities in a Race with Time: Progress and Poverty in America's Renewing Cities* (New York: Random House, 1967).

[13] Park H. Martin, "Pittsburgh's Comprehensive Improvement Program," American Society of Civic Engineers, *Transactions*, 121 (1956), reprint, 887; Pennsylvania Economy League, *Newsletter for Western Pennsylvania*, 26 (May–June 1960), 3. These values had plummeted to an all-time low of $961 million by 1947, following the construction moratorium of the Depression and World War II.

Point before Smoke Control, 1936.

enterprise system itself has sought and established in Pittsburgh
a partnership between private business and all levels of government."[14] The irony of the environmental change process in twentieth century Pittsburgh was not that it ultimately hinged upon
constructive public intervention, but that use of public resources
was so closely identified with the corporate welfare.

Point renewal was essential to the physical and economic rehabilitation of the entire 330-acre CBD, or Golden Triangle. The
creation of a park at the Point to commemorate Fort Pitt and
Fort Duquesne had been advocated in the 1930's, when the City
Planning Commission acquired title to the separate land parcels
coinciding with the sites of the historic forts. The Historical
Society of Western Pennsylvania supported the idea of a national
park, as did Mayor Scully. In 1938 the Planning Commission
decided to prepare sketch plans, and in 1940 the mayor appointed a Point Park Commission. It proposed that the park
should "take the form of a National Historic Site" and launched
negotiations with the National Park Service.[15] The war then
intervened.

[14] Wallace Richards, "Pittsburgh's Thrilling Civic Renaissance," *American
City*, **65** (July 1950), 155.
[15] *Report of the Point Park Commission, Pittsburgh, Part One* (December
31, 1943), *passim*.

Golden Triangle, 1947.

Under the direction of the ACCD, beginning in 1945, interest shifted from a national to a state park; and the Conference broke the deadlock that had long delayed any kind of action. Over past decades, no plan "succeeded in getting the historical and highway interests to agree on a practical. compromise. For the historical promoters the restoration of Fort Pitt in its entirety was paramount. For the highway planners the preservation of the existing traffic routes including the bridges at the apex of the Point was essential."[16] A plan prepared by Ralph Griswold and Charles Stotz for the Pittsburgh Regional Planning Association in 1945, which depended upon removal of the bridges, was accepted by Governor Martin as the basis for a state park. At the request of the State Department of Forests and Waters, the ACCD, acting through a Point Park Committee under Arthur Van Buskirk, assumed responsibility for coordination and development of the project. By 1949, acquisition of the 36 acres was completed at a cost of $7 million, and demolition began on 15

[16] Ralph E. Griswold, "From Fort Pitt to Point Park: A Turning Point in the Physical Planning of Pittsburgh," *Landscape Architecture*, **46** (July 1956), 197.

acres of freight yards, elevated freight-railway tracks and termi-
nal, some 26 commercial buildings, and the old Exposition Hall.[17]

Point Park marked the beginning of the alliance between the
Mellon-backed ACCD and the Democratic political machine
headed by David Lawrence, elected to the first of four terms as
Mayor in 1945.[18] To aid the Republican candidate in the 1945
mayoralty campaign, the state administration delayed announce-
ment until October of plans for the park and the first segment of
a limited-access highway that would eventually link the Pennsylvania Turnpike and Greater Pittsburgh Airport via downtown
Pittsburgh. Lawrence, however, expressed delight that the state
was aiding the city, and simply identified himself with the park
and expressway projects.[19] After the election, meetings were held
between Lawrence, Mellon, Van Buskirk, Martin, Richards,
County Commissioner Kane, and Attorney General (later Governor) James Duff.[20] By 1946, the civic coalition was established
and the campaign for smoke control launched. Lawrence staked
his political future on this issue; Mellon and the ACCD were
equally committed as far as the economic future of Pittsburgh
was concerned. If Point Park served as a catalyst for the formation of the civic coalition, smoke control demonstrated its effectiveness.

Lawrence inherited a smoke control law passed in 1941. Although the city council had abolished the Bureau of Smoke Control in 1939, councilman Abraham L. Wolk began a crusade for
new legislation.[21] The St. Louis smoke control ordinance of 1940

[17] According to Griswold, a prominent Pittsburgh landscape architect, Stotz
was the "architect and historian" who insisted on the design necessity for
removing the existing bridges. (*Ibid.*, 197–198.) On the origins and evolution of Point Park see also, Charles M. Stotz, "Point State Park: Birth Place
of Pittsburgh," *Carnegie Magazine*, 38 (January 1964), 15–20; *Pittsburgh
Press*, December 28, 1945; *Pittsburgh Post-Gazette*, November 15, 1945,
May 2, 1946, February 14, 1948, April 17, 1951, September 16, 1952, and
January 16, 1964.
[18] Lawrence, who served as Governor of Pennsylvania (1959–1963), did
not complete his last term as mayor.
[19] Lawrence, "Rebirth," 419 (cited in footnote 12).
[20] Alfred Steinberg, "Pittsburgh, a New City," *National Municipal Review*,
44 (March 1955), 129; Lowe, *Cities in a Race with Time*, 132.
[21] "Recommendation Offered to Meet Pittsburgh's Big Smoke Problem,"

became the inspiration and model for Pittsburgh, where a strong
alliance formed by the winter of 1941. Dr. I. Hope Alexander,
Pittsburgh's health director, journeyed to St. Louis at the request
of Mayor Scully and the city council. "Photographs and the evidence of Dr. Alexander's own eyes left no doubt about it—St.
Louis is now as spotless as pre-War Rotterdam. And the experts
agree that Pittsburgh can do what St. Louis has done. . . ."[22]

The Civic Club, Allegheny County Medical Society, and
League of Women Voters endorsed smoke control.[23] Gilbert Love
of the *Pittsburgh Press* publicized the St. Louis experience and
fact that "thousands of prospective citizens . . . have been lost
to Pittsburgh because they did not like the idea of living and
bringing up their families in atmospheric filth." Local corporations had difficulty recruiting employees, and "often a valuable
man will quit a Pittsburgh establishment, or seek a transfer, for
the sole purpose of securing more pleasant living conditions for
himself and his family."[24] Although these arguments had been
used since the early twentieth century, they became more per-
suasive by the late 1930's when the Golden Triangle and region
confronted the Depression and bleak implications of economic
"maturity."

Mayor Scully and the council visited St. Louis in February,
1941.[25] The Mayor then appointed a Smoke Commission under
the chairmanship of Wolk. The Commission advanced several
arguments on behalf of smoke control. Atmospheric pollution
produced a high incidence of pneumonia, sinus ailments, and
fibrosis of lung tissue. It destroyed vegetation and resulted in
abnormally expensive cleaning bills. Not least important, "practically everyone has heard of persons who have refused to accept
positions here because of Pittsburgh's reputation as a 'dirty city.'"
Smoke control might even be the key to economic diversification.

Greater Pittsburgh, **22** (March 1941), 23; "Smoke Out," *Bulletin Index,*
118 (June 26, 1941), 6.

[22] *Bulletin Index,* **118** (February 13, 1941), 6.

[23] *Pittsburgh Press,* January 27, 1941; *Pittsburgh Post-Gazette,* February 10,
February 19, 1941.

[24] *Pittsburgh Press,* January 31, 1941.

[25] *Pittsburgh Post-Gazette,* February 19, 1941. They were accompanied by
Dr. David A. Kurtzman, director of research for the Pennsylvania Economy
League.

"With proper promotion, a considerable growth of smaller, lighter industries might well follow the elimination of the smoke nuisance here."[26] The Commission recommended, and the council enacted, an ordinance based on the simple, but effective St. Louis policy. Consumers had to use smokeless fuel, or else install "fuel-burning equipment which has been found to prevent the production of smoke."[27] In contrast to previous legislation, private homes and multiple-dwellings with less than six units would have to comply. War-induced fuel shortages and production demands, however, prevented enforcement for the duration of the war.

A United Smoke Council, organized in 1945, soon became an affiliate of the ACCD.[28] Its objectives included enforcement of the 1941 legislation and extension of smoke control to the county. The Council supported Mayor Lawrence's decision to require industry, railroads, and commercial buildings to comply by October 1, 1946, followed by residential dwellings one year later. Lawrence depended upon the ACCD to prevent obstruction from the coal companies. "Richard King Mellon and his associates in the Allegheny Conference," Lawrence observed, "gave their strong support. Without them I would not have been successful. I had not much influence with the Consolidation Coal Company, while Mr. Mellon's prestige with them was great."[29] Lawrence and the ACCD also overcame opposition from the soft-coal miners. John Busarello, president of District No. 5, United Mine Workers, complained of a conspiracy to "reduce the market for Pittsburgh district coal." Someone, he insisted, "is trying to get

[26] Report of the Mayor's Commission for the Elimination of Smoke (1941), 11.

[27] Ibid., 14. The campaign for the smoke control ordinance had been launched by the St. Louis Post-Dispatch in 1939. Mayor Bernard Dickmann appointed a citizen's committee headed by James L. Ford, Jr., a banker. In its report of 1940, the committee recommended legislation that required smokeless fuel or use of effective mechanical equipment. A $300,000 municipal revolving fund was established for the purchase and distribution of smokeless fuel in the event of scarcity. This was not needed, despite a boycott of St. Louis by Illinois mining interests. See Pittsburgh Press, November 8, 1945; Pittsburgh Post-Gazette, July 31, 1946; "How St. Louis, Led by the Post-Dispatch, Solved the City's Acute Smoke Problem," in Hal Burton (ed.), The City Fights Back (New York: Citadel Press, 1954), Appendix D.

[28] Pittsburgh Press, October 15, December 23, 1945.

[29] Lawrence, "Rebirth," 386 (cited in footnote 12).

Jones and Laughlin Steel, 2nd Avenue.

the people of Allegheny County to buy their coal outside of the
county and someone else is trying to get the people to throw out
their furnaces and burn gas. They are trying to take work from
our miners."[30] Although smoke control was not a conspiracy, the
mine workers' fears were not groundless. Smoke control depended, in large degree, upon reducing use of the district's high-
volatile bituminous coal for engines and domestic heating. It
hastened the conversion to diesel locomotives, and to gas in
homes and apartments.

The influence of the Pennsylvania RR in Harrisburg posed the
chief obstacle to extension of smoke control to the county.
Enabling legislation for county smoke control, passed in 1943,
had exempted the railroads. The ACCD sponsored a bill in 1947

[30] *Pittsburgh Press,* December 21, 1945; *Pittsburgh Sun-Telegraph,* December 21, 1945. Lawrence's smoke control program was vehemently criticized
by councilman Edward J. Leonard, Friend of the "Little Joes" who presumably would suffer from higher fuel costs. Head of the Plasterers' Union
and active in the Pittsburgh Central Labor Union, Leonard unsuccessfully
opposed Lawrence in the 1949 democratic primary. See Lawrence, "Rebirth," 397.

that brought them under control; an understanding, presumably, had been reached with the Pennsylvania RR. The Conference delegation in Harrisburg was surprised and infuriated to find that the Pennsylvania's lobbyist, Rufus Flynn, nonetheless opposed the legislation. Wallace Richards contacted Mellon who informed the president of the Pennsylvania that other railroads would be delighted to handle his business. Benjamin Fairless of United States Steel also demanded that the Pennsylvania cooperate. The enabling legislation passed.[31]

The ACCD then exerted its influence on behalf of a county-wide smoke control law. The United Smoke Council organized smoke-abatement committees in each municipality, sponsored educational programs on the harmful effects of smoke, and circulated petitions requesting the county commissioners to enact an ordinance. The commissioners appointed a 17-member Smoke Abatement Advisory Committee under Edward Weidlein to prepare the legislation, which was passed in 1949. In 1957 the county absorbed the Pittsburgh Health Department, whose Bureau of Smoke Regulation had enforced the City ordinance. A new comprehensive regulation, administered by the County Bureau of Air Pollution Control, was passed in 1960.[32]

By that date the urgency and sense of crisis had passed. The smoke control legislation of the 1940's had achieved its purpose;

[31] Theodore L. Hazlett, quoted in *Pittsburgh Press*, December 10, 1953; Park H. Martin, "How the Pittsburgh Program is Being Accomplished," (typed, ACCD, files), March 28, 1951, 7–8; Lawrence, "Rebirth," 390.

[32] "Prescription for Pittsburgh," *Bulletin Index*, 131 (November 1947), 10; Martin, "How the Pittsburgh Program is Being Accomplished," 8; *Cinderella City: How Community Action Transformed Pittsburgh's Smoke-Stained Identity*, National Association of Manufacturers, Current Issue Series, No. 12, Economic Problems Department (December 1962), 8–10; Allegheny County, Bureau of Smoke Control, *Report of Activities for the Year Ending June 1, 1950*, 2; David N. Kuhn, "Progress on the Smoke Front," *Allegheny Conference Digest*, 1 (September 1946), 8.

A key strategy in enforcing smoke control had been to concentrate upon coal dealers rather than private consumers. It became illegal for dealers to sell high volatile coal for use in hand-fired furnaces. In the Pittsburgh ordinance, low volatile coal was defined "as containing less than 20% volatile matter on a dry basis." See Pittsburgh, Department of Public Health, Bureau of Smoke Prevention, *Report on Stationary Stacks* (1946), 3; *Ibid.* (1947), 6.

it eliminated the blatant ash and soot pollution that required street lighting at high noon, and thus enabled the civic coalition to proceed with its reconstruction program. Subsequently, progress under county auspices has been uneven. Gaseous and microdust pollution is extensive, including high levels of nitrogen and sulfur dioxide.[33] Certain sections of the city, like Squirrel Hill and especially Hazelwood, still suffer at times from a thick, malodorous smog and a quick settling layer of black dust. Generous provision for staggered enforcement in the county legislation has permitted the use of obsolete equipment in steel plants. Pockets of old-style, thick grey-black smoke still existed in the 1960's in the river valley milltowns.[34]

As vital in the creation of the reverse welfare state as Point Park, and elimination of the most visible atmospheric pollution, was flood control. Renewal of the Golden Triangle could not progress without assurance to investors that a catastrophe like the St. Patrick's Day Flood of 1936 would never be repeated.

[33] Henry W. Pierce, "New Air Pollution Perils Pittsburgh," *Pittsburgh Post-Gazette*, November 23, 1967.

[34] The Renaissance effort included an attack on water as well as air pollution. An Allegheny County Sanitary Authority was established in 1946, and reorganized in 1955 as a joint City-County agency. Its goal was the construction of many miles of sewers to carry wastes to a central treatment plant. The Authority grew out of studies and recommendations of the ACCD. See ACCD, *Presents*, 21; Edward R. Weidlein, "Allegheny Conference Progress," *Allegheny Conference Digest*, 2 (June 1947), 2; "A Sewage Subway to Cleaner Streams," *Greater Pittsburgh*, 38 (April 1956), 22–24.

The region's waterways suffer from a combination of acid discharges from strip-mines and industrial wastes. Despite state and local regulations, and the efforts of the Sanitary Authority, pollution remains widespread. The following episode is typical in the Pittsburgh region. "North Versailles Twp. Water Authority officials have blamed the U. S. Steel Corp for tainting the water supply of their 15,000 residents and have issued a stern 'desist' letter. The foul-tasting water appeared at the water plant intakes on the Monongahela River Feb. 16 and lingered in the system for three days. Although State inspectors earlier said a phenol compound had been dumped at night, they said they could not identify the violators. But township officials, tired of periodic dumpings, yesterday named the source as Clairton Works of U. S. Steel." *Pittsburgh Press*, March 1, 1968. Drinking water, generally, in the Pittsburgh area is a strange assortment of colors, flavors, and contents. It may not be lethal, but it sometimes looks and tastes as if it is.

Fifth Avenue, at Market, looking toward Jenkins Arcade, 1936 flood.

Most of downtown had been inundated by waters that "crested at a record 46 feet."[35] The Pittsburgh Chamber of Commerce, long interested in flood control, had initiated a campaign to have the federal government build a series of dams in the Upper Ohio Valley. Their construction began in the 1930's, but "pressure had to be applied continually on each session of Congress for appropriations." The system progressed rapidly after World War II, when the Chamber's promotional efforts were reinforced by the ACCD and the *Pittsburgh Press*.[36]

The projects discussed—Point Park, smoke control, and flood control—suggest that the creation of the reverse welfare state depended upon the resources of all levels of government. One of the great strengths of the civic coalition was its tactical flexibility. It did not hesitate to use any administrative expedient like the special authority, or to seek assistance from any tier of government. The Federal role became more prominent after the

---

[35] *Pittsburgh Press*, December 13, 1953, supplement.
[36] *Ibid.*; "Civic Regeneration," *Greater Pittsburgh*, **28** (September 1947), 9; ACCD, *Presents*, 20. Between 1936 and 1956 the Corps of Engineers constructed 10 flood-control reservoirs in the Upper Ohio Valley.

Housing Act of 1949; the success of the civic coalition before then was based, in large measure, upon its influence in Harrisburg.

Mellon and his associates in the ACCD linked the civic coalition to the Republican leadership of the county and state. This was critical in light of the need for state enabling legislation as in smoke control, or state funds as in Point Park and related highway-bridge construction.[37] In the fall of 1946, the executive committee of the ACCD authorized the preparation of a state legislative program on behalf of Pittsburgh. Ten bills, the "Pittsburgh Package," were devised in cooperation with the Pennsylvania Economic League, Pittsburgh Regional Planning Association, and Lawrence administration. As usual, the ACCD attempted to create an advance bipartisan consensus. It obtained the support of Democratic County Commissioner Kane, Republican Governor Duff, and the Republican and Democratic County Chairmen. Eight of the bills were introduced jointly in the House and Senate by Republican and Democratic legislators from Allegheny County; the other two were presented as "administrative measures of the City of Pittsburgh with assurance of the support of the opposition party."[38]

Eight of the ten bills passed.[39] County smoke control, discussed previously, was authorized. Another enabled Pittsburgh to create a public parking authority. A third permitted the county to establish a transit and traffic commission to study mass transportation. The Penn-Lincoln Parkway linking downtown with the Pennsylvania turnpike was expedited by freeing the City "from the burden of consequential damages in building express highways in Pittsburgh." The remaining bills authorized the county to build waste disposal facilities, broadened the tax base of Pittsburgh and other communities, created a Department of Parks

[37] The state also contributed $600,000 toward construction of the Greater Pittsburgh Airport, opened for commercial airline use in 1952.
[38] ACCD, *Executive Director's Report*, Third Annual Meeting, September 16, 1947 (mimeographed), 2; Marshall Stalley, "Pittsburgh and the Allegheny Conference: Effort Toward a Unified Community Program for the Region," *Landscape Architecture*, 38 (July 1948), 150; Harry Henderson, "You'd Never Know Pittsburgh," *Collier's*, 131 (May 30, 1953), 60.
[39] One of the bills that died in committee would have amended the Public Utility Commission Act to allow Allegheny County to file complaints before the Public Utilities Commission.

and Recreation in Pittsburgh, and expanded the County Planning Commission's control over suburban subdivision plans.[40]

Point Park and the Penn-Lincoln Parkway, smoke and flood control, the Pittsburgh Package, and legislation in 1945 and 1947 that permitted insurance companies to invest in redevelopment areas paved the way for Golden Triangle renewal. Pennsylvania had already enacted a housing and redevelopment law in 1945; it enabled municipalities to establish redevelopment authorities that could acquire and clear land in areas certified as blighted by the city planning commission. Lawrence singled out Van Buskirk and Richards as "among the first Pittsburghers to see its opportunities."[41] They visualized, in particular, the possibilities arising out of the fire of March, 1946, which swept the upper Point, destroying the Wabash RR facilities (owned by the Pennsylvania and West Virginia RR). About this time (according to Lawrence), Van Buskirk and Richards arrived at City Hall; they suggested that Pittsburgh establish an Urban Redevelopment Authority (URA), and that Lawrence appoint himself as chairman.[42] The composition of the URA, established in November, both exemplified and solidified the civic coalition. Van Buskirk served as vice-chairman. The other members included Lester Perry of the Carnegie-Illinois Steel Corporation; department store magnate Edgar Kaufmann; and Democratic city councilman William Alvah Stewart. Lawrence's secretary, John Robins, became the URA's first executive director.

In the months between the March, 1946 conflagration at the Point, and the establishment of the URA in November, the ACCD launched negotiations leading to the 23-acre Gateway Center adjoining Point Park. During the summer of 1946, Van Buskirk, Richards, Martin, and Charles J. Graham, president of the Pittsburgh and West Virginia RR, journeyed to New York in the hopes of interesting the Metropolitan Life Insurance Company. This proved unsuccessful and Graham suggested they try

---

[40] Stalley, "Pittsburgh and the Allegheny Conference," 150; Marshall Stalley, "Horizons Beyond the Smoke," *National Municipal Review*, 36 (November 1947), 559; Dr. Robert H. Doherty, "The Pittsburgh of Tomorrow," *Greater Pittsburgh*, 28 (March 1947), 18–19.

[41] Lawrence, "Rebirth," 433 (cited in footnote 12).

[42] *Ibid.*, 430–431.

Thomas J. Parkinson, president of Equitable Life, who responded favorably.[43] The City Planning Commission in March, 1947 certified the 59-acre Point (including the 36-acre Point Park) as eligible for redevelopment. The URA negotiated a contract with Equitable involving no federal aid. The project was officially approved by the mayor and council in 1950, when construction began.

Gateway Center was the most dramatic expression of the reverse welfare state in Pittsburgh. The extensive utilization of public powers and resources between 1945–1950 made Gateway Center, and thus reconstruction of the Golden Triangle, possible. It illustrated the tactics of the civic coalition in generating large-scale environmental change. These included use of the public authority mechanism or any administrative expedient that could link Pittsburgh with government assistance at any level. Gateway Center also depended upon the civic coalition's access to professional and technical skills—architectural, planning, engineering, and legal. Finally, Gateway Center was the product of an extraordinary combination of prestige and power, one that could induce Equitable and local corporations to invest millions in the future of the CBD and break the deadlocks that had obstructed environmental change in the past. Equitable's investment, for example, was contingent not only upon smoke and flood control, but guaranteed long-term leases for 60 percent of the projected office space. Through Van Buskirk, therefore, "nine of the largest companies in Pittsburgh, such as Westinghouse, Jones and Laughlin, Pittsburgh Plate Glass Company, were drawn into negotiations for twenty-year leases. The whole program was put together before a single shovel of earth was turned."[44] A long-time obstacle to Golden Triangle renewal, eliminated through the influence of the ACCD, was the "tussle between the divergent real estate interests of the lower end and of the upper portions

[43] Ibid., 432.

[44] Leland Hazard, How Citizens and Officers of Pittsburgh Worked Together to Solve Metropolitan Problems (mimeographed address, Conference on Metropolitan St. Louis Problems, Washington University, St. Louis, November 14, 1952), 12. And, according to Theodore L. Hazlett, "Equitable wanted to know definitely if the smoke ordinance was going to be effective. When we answered 'yes,' Gateway was made . . ." Quoted in Pittsburgh Press, December 10, 1953.

Point Park, Gateway Center, 1965.

of the Golden Triangle."[45] Edgar Kaufmann (a member of the URA) acquiesced in the plans for Gateway Center despite the fact that a competitor, Horne's Department Store, was located closer to the Point end of downtown.

Gateway Center, the catalyst of the downtown building revival, included three 20–24 story, cruciform, stainless steel office buildings opened in 1952 and 1953. These were followed by a state office building (1957), Bell Telephone Building (1958), 750-car underground garage (1959), Hilton Hotel (1959), another 22-story office building (1960), IBM Building (1963), and 27-story Gateway Towers luxury apartments (1964). Further up the Triangle, off William Penn Place, two more skyscraper office buildings arose in the early 1950's: the stainless-steel U. S. Steel-Mellon Bank Building and the aluminum-sheathed Alcoa Building. These structures overlook Mellon Square Park, a small but

[45] Hazard, "How Citizens and Officers of Pittsburgh Worked Together . . . ," 11–12. The sponsors of Gateway center also overcame opposition from owners of existing office buildings and realtors. According to one account, opposition of realtors was eliminated by hiring them as property acquisition agents. Lowe, *Cities in a Race with Time*, 142.

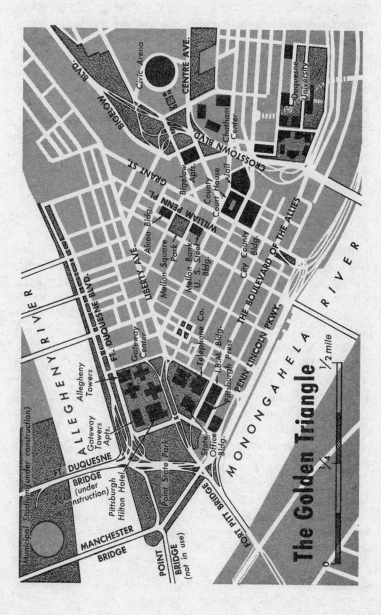

The Golden Triangle

Municipal Stadium (under construction)

ALLEGHENY RIVER

FT. DUQUESNE

BRIDGE (under construction)

MANCHESTER BRIDGE

Pittsburgh Hilton Hotel

POINT BRIDGE (not in use)

Point State Park

FORT PITT BRIDGE

FT. DUQUESNE BLVD.

Gateway Center

Allegheny Towers

Gateway Towers Apts.

LIBERTY AVE.

Alcoa Bldg.

Mellon Square Park

Telephone Co.

I.B.M. Bldg.

Pittsburgh Press

State Office Bldg.

PENN LINCOLN PKWY.

Mellon Bank– U. S. Steel Bldg.

WILLIAM PENN PL.

GRANT ST.

Bigelow Apts.

County Court House

Jail

City County Bldg.

THE BOULEVARD OF THE ALLIES

CROSSTOWN BLVD.

BIGELOW BLVD.

Civic Arena

CENTRE AVE.

Chatham Center

Duquesne University

MONONGAHELA RIVER

0   ¼   ½ mile

attractive addition to the downtown landscape. It originated when three Mellon Foundations announced a $4 million gift to the City in 1949 for an underground garage topped by a block-size parklet.[46] This complex of buildings and park along William Penn Place testified dramatically to the determination of the Mellon family to invest in the commercial future of Pittsburgh.

The URA, which had assembled the land for Gateway Center, was the first of a series of special authorities that helped to forge the reverse welfare state in Pittsburgh. The same mechanism was used to cope with parking and transportation problems that had plagued the CBD for decades. At the request of the ACCD, the Pittsburgh Regional Planning Association prepared a report on downtown parking. Published in 1946, it led to the enabling legislation for a Parking Authority included in the Pittsburgh Package of 1947. The report noted that the automobile had become the dominant form of transportation in the CBD by 1937. The precipitous decline of property values and closing down of many small businesses were related to the "lack of parking space." Indeed, the issue had the profoundest implications for the future of the Golden Triangle and, therefore, the city. "Are we to try to preserve our cities as we know them, or are the natural forces of decentralization . . . to be permitted to go along unchecked by remedial efforts?"[47] As Park Martin explained, "If 'Downtown' is to continue to hold its own with suburban shopping centers, it must have sufficient well located parking lots or garages." Private enterprise, however, could not establish the coordinated system of parking facilities upon which the survival of the CBD depended.[48] Within the next few years, the Pittsburgh Parking Au-

[46] Mellon Square Park opened in 1955. On its origins, see "Magnificent Square in the Triangle," *Greater Pittsburgh*, 37 (October 1955), 19–22, 62–63; ACCD, *Presents*, 9.

[47] *Parking Study of the Pittsburgh Central Business District* (prepared by the Pittsburgh Regional Planning Association for the Allegheny Conference on Community Development, 1945–1946), 62, 67.

[48] Park H. Martin, *Problems of 'Downtown'* (mimeographed address, Cavendish Trading Corporation Meeting, White Sulphur Springs, Virginia, September 15, 1955), 7. The Pittsburgh "theory," according to Martin, was that off-street parking was an extension of the street surface; this implied a public responsibility.

thority constructed more than half a dozen strategically located garages.

The ACCD maintained that an "efficient mass transportation system" was equally important for the preservation of the CBD and "general economic well-being of the area." It viewed a Transit Authority as the only "possible means . . . for consolidating and modernizing the existing carriers." Along with the Regional Planning Association and Pennsylvania Economy League, the ACCD sponsored a mass transit study, published in 1949. The report complained of the historic ineptitude of private transit management in Pittsburgh, leading to "duplication of routes, competition, and a multiplicity of types, sizes and ages of equipment."[49] Key recommendations included unified ownership and management of mass transit in Allegheny County, and substitution of buses for street cars (as Robert Moses had proposed in 1939). The Port Authority Transit acquired the properties in 1964, and began the large-scale substitution of buses for trolleys in 1967.[50] Two more authorities—Auditorium and Stadium— were established in connection with URA projects.

The URA, through Gateway Center, had played a major role in the reconstruction of the Golden Triangle. Between 1950, when Gateway Center was begun, and the mid-1960's, more than 25 percent of the 330-acre Triangle was rebuilt. But the economic viability of the central business district depended ultimately upon the broader metropolitan economy; the URA program, therefore, was closely tied to the expansion needs of industrial and commercial firms. The URA's corporate welfare program, supplemented by extensive luxury housing construction, was understandably favored by municipal authorities in quest of an improved tax base.

[49] *Mass Transportation Study of Pittsburgh and Allegheny County* (sponsored jointly by Allegheny Conference on Community Development, Pittsburgh Regional Planning Association, and Pennsylvania Economy League, September 1949), II, Park Martin, "Forward," 1; Edward J. Magee, *The Rebirth of a Region* (mimeographed address, Pittsburgh Builders Exchange, October 18, 1960), 3.

[50] Edward Jensen, "Pittsburgh's Venture into Public Transit," *Pittsburgh Business Review*, 37 (August 1967), 1–6.

By 1967, 19 renewal projects were completed or under construction. These encompassed approximately 1500 acres (765 clearance, 379 conservation-rehabilitation, and the remainder vacant land reclamation). Of the total acreage, 465 acres were committed to industrial reuse, and another 103 acres to commercial-office reuse. The total public costs were estimated at $171.5 million (including a federal share of $112 million spread over 8 of the projects). According to the URA, approximately $125 million in tax assessments had been restored in renewal areas by 1967, 50 industrial firms had been accommodated in new or modernized facilities, and 55,000 persons worked in firms located in renewal areas (including 22,000 in Gateway Center compared to fewer than 4000 before 1948). The renewal process, the URA emphasized, was a "key factor in the continuing development of Downtown Pittsburgh. Some 60 major new structures erected there since 1949 have enabled the City to solidify its position as one of the nation's three leading administrative centers of corporate headquarters." Closely related to this achievement, "renewal has helped stabilize the City's supply of jobs, particularly in managerial, administrative, professional and skilled industrial occupations."[51]

No less than three URA projects were devised for the benefit of Jones and Laughlin Steel. J & L decided in 1948 to modernize its South Side works and construct eleven new open hearth furnaces. Appreciation of property values in the area halted land acquisition and the Company requested assistance from the URA. The city council approved a 32-acre redevelopment plan in 1949.[52] In 1952 the URA and council again responded to the expansion needs of J & L with 74-acre and 13-acre clearance projects (Hazelwood and Scotch Bottom, respectively).[53]

The appointment of Robert Pease as executive director of the URA in 1958 led to extensive commercial, industrial, and luxury

[51] Pittsburgh, Urban Redevelopment Authority, *Digest of the Urban Renewal Program* (September 1967) (mimeographed data sheet). Unless otherwise noted, data on URA operations are drawn from this source and from Robert B. Pease, *Report on Renewal—1966.*

[52] For a detailed account of the J & L renewal project, see David W. Elliott, "Urban Redevelopment—An Industrial Application," unpublished M.A., University of Pittsburgh, 1953.

[53] None of the J & L projects was federally aided.

apartment renewal on the Lower North Side.[54] Chateau Street
West in the Manchester district (1960) (refers to date of approval by the city council) encompassed 98 acres, and was
described by Pease as a "demonstration of the use of urban
renewal as a key tool in industrial development" within the "con-
gested central city." Woods Run (1967) in Upper Manchester,
a 126-acre extension of Chateau Street West, also emphasized
industrial reuse. The 103-acre Allegheny Center (1961) included
a large shopping center, garage, townhouses, and apartments.
The adjoining 5-acre Allegheny South (1964) featured a new
post office and gas plant to service Allegheny Center. The 84-
acre stadium project (1963) will provide a new arena for the
Pittsburgh Pirates and Steelers. The 56-acre Reedsale-Ridge
(1965), next to the stadium area, was designed partly for industrial reuse but primarily to secure the right-of-way for a link
in the North Side Expressway system. Pease extended urban
renewal to Pittsburgh's West End as well as to the North Side.
The vast 327-acre Chartiers Valley project (1965) demonstrated
once again, according to Pease, "the urban renewal process . . .
employed . . . to generate economic growth." Vacant, city-
owned land and Pennsylvania Railroad property will be transformed into a "modern industrial park."

A group of URA projects was designed to assist Pittsburgh's
major educational and medical institutions. DeSota-Thackeray
(1953) cleared 3 acres in Oakland for an addition to Children's
Hospital and construction of the University of Pittsburgh's
School of Public Health. Centre-Morgan (1953) cleared another
26 acres in Oakland for a University of Pittsburgh physical education complex. Bluff Street (1962) devoted 43 acres to apartments and new Duquesne University buildings. Allegheny General (1963) on the North Side provided Allegheny General Hospital with 19 acres for staff housing and other facilities.

Sheraden Park (1963) was the only project devoted exclusively
to construction of moderate-cost housing. ACTION-Housing
built 188 row-house units on the 46-acre site. The 117-acre Homewood North (1966), and East Liberty (1960, 1963) projects were
the first to emphasize conservation and rehabilitation. Combined

[54] Trained as a civil engineer at the Carnegie Institute of Technology (now
Carnegie-Mellon University), Pease joined the URA in 1953.

into a single 254-acre renewal project in 1964, East Liberty included new housing, extensive road improvements, commercial rehabilitation, and pedestrian shopping malls.[55]

Low-cost housing, clearly, was an insignificant element in the renewal process. By 1966, at least 5400 families had been displaced, while 1719 new dwelling units had been built or were under construction. Most of these were high rent; 594 units in the Lower Hill, 311 in Gateway Center, and 350 in Allegheny Center. An additional 3610 were projected, but these included 540 luxury units in the Lower Hill and 1240 in Allegheny Center. Another 1273 units were proposed for East Liberty, supplementing the 296-unit Pennley Park North apartments. There was, however, a perceptible change of emphasis in URA policy during the 1960's. Homewood North and East Liberty not only substituted rehabilitation-conservation for total clearance, but involved a greater degree of citizen participation. Along with Sheraden Park, they indicated some concern for at least moderate-cost housing. These trends were the outgrowth, in part, of increasing Negro resistance to bulldozer renewal and, most concretely, the resentment generated by the Lower Hill redevelopment.

The turbulent Lower Hill scheme pivoted around a civic auditorium. Plans published in 1947 and 1951 by the Pittsburgh Regional Planning Association and URA, respectively, proposed a combined convention hall and sports arena along with residential apartments for the site. Edgar J. Kaufmann became especially enamored of a civic auditorium with a retractable roof, which would also house the Pittsburgh Civic Light Opera. This was proposed in another plan prepared by the ACCD and released in 1953. State enabling legislation that year was followed by the creation of the Public Auditorium Authority of Pittsburgh and Allegheny County in 1954. The Edgar J. Kaufmann Charitable Trust contributed $1 million toward construction of the arena.[56]

55 *Pittsburgh Post-Gazette*, November 4, 1967; Robert B. Pease, "A Community Shapes Its Future: East Liberty's Role in Renewal," *Greater Pittsburgh*, 47 (May 1965), 12–14.

56 *Pittsburgh Press*, October 30, 1947, May 26, 1951; *Pittsburgh Sun-Telegraph*, February 4, 1952; Herbick and Held, *Pittsburgh Quote* (1967), n.p.; ACCD, *Presents*, 12–13.

Civic Arena, 1961.

Although the City Planning Commission had certified the 95-acre Lower Hill for redevelopment in 1950, uncertainties over financing and planning delayed council approval until 1955. Demolition began in 1956, displacing 1551 (mostly Negro) families and 413 businesses. The $22 million, domed Civic Arena with retractable roof opened in 1961. Glistening in isolated splendor amid expressways and parking lots, it turned out to be something of a civic incubus. For the Negro community, it has been a highly visible symbol of old-style renewal, indifferent to the housing needs and preferences of low-income families. The atrociously planned parking lot causes long delays in exiting after a major event. And, as Lewis Mumford warned in 1956, "After the first novelty wears off, it is not the roof but the musical performances and the general comfort of the patrons that will make people come to the auditorium."[57] By any criterion, the retractable roof was a disaster. It added enormously to the expense and is hardly ever practical to open because of weather,

[57] Lewis Mumford, "Memorandum on Civic and Educational Policy in Pittsburgh," unpublished, July 11, 1956, 8.

wind, or noise. The roof did not improve an acoustics problem that makes musical entertainment at the Civic Arena a painful experience for all concerned.

Also painful were the confusion and delays affecting other phases of the Lower Hill redevelopment. Webb and Knapp had been awarded the contract for residential construction in 1959, but the 396-unit Forbes Tower (first of the projected Washington Plaza Apartments) was not completed until 1964; the Aluminum Company of America had taken over the property from the floundering Webb and Knapp firm the previous year. Downtown hotel operators instituted legal proceedings to prevent construction of a motor hotel in the Lower Hill. The URA was sustained by the courts in 1962–1963, and construction finally began in 1964 on a revised and expanded scheme known at Chatham Center: two high-rise buildings that included apartments, a motor hotel, offices, garage, and movie theater. The Crosstown Expressway linking Boulevard of the Allies and Bigelow was also completed in 1964.[58]

It had been assumed that the Civic Arena would constitute one unit in a broader cultural center, including a symphony hall, theater, and possibly an art museum. But an impasse developed. The Negro community resolutely opposed further large-scale clearance and insisted upon a voice in any planning for the Hill district. On the other hand, the persons "most needed want to make certain that the proposed cultural center is not built next to a seething slum; they want renewal for the Upper Hill to protect their donations." Meanwhile, a local newspaper editorialized, "The men of the Renaissance have been unable to produce anything but a crop of weeds on 9.2 acres of prime public land next to the Civic Arena."[59]

The civic coalition experienced greater success in the economic sphere. Along with the URA and other public authorities, the City Planning Department labored to create an environment

[58] "Lower Hill: An Impressive Timetable," *Greater Pittsburgh*, 41 (September 1959), 13–14; *Pittsburgh Post-Gazette*, September 29, 1964; Herbick and Held, *Pittsburgh Quote;* Pease, "Report on Renewal, 4; URA, *Report of Progress* (January 1964), 8–10.
[59] *Pittsburgh Press*, May 14, 1961; *Pittsburgh Point*, April 6, 1967. Also, *Pittsburgh Post-Gazette*, July 5, 1968.

favorable to corporate enterprise. It became particularly active in economic planning and promotion in the 1960's, sounding at times like an adjunct to the Chamber of Commerce. "The rebuilding of Pittsburgh," the Department maintained, "hinges on a fundamental concept in economics: IF PITTSBURGH IS TO GROW IT MUST HAVE A SOUND EMPLOYMENT AND ECONOMIC BASE!" The Department, therefore, had to develop "an aggressive program directed toward keeping the City's industry and assisting in industrial plant expansion."[60] It completed a detailed tabulation of land and floor space in the Golden Triangle in 1960, and cooperated with the Regional Planning Association in developing a general plan for the area. Other activities included a field survey of 1100 industrial firms to compile information "vital to assisting future expansion and solving the immediate operating programs of industry." The Department engaged in studies of industrial park sites, and aided firms to expand by vacating streets and alleys, allowing zoning variances, and assisting in the sale of publicly-owned property.[61]

A major premise behind the creation of the reverse welfare state, as the activities of the URA and City Planning Commission suggest, was that market forces alone would neither induce nor protect investment in the Golden Triangle; and they would not invigorate a sluggish regional economy. Planned intervention —public and private—was needed to improve the Pittsburgh region's competitive situation. To help achieve this goal, the Regional Industrial Development Corporation (RIDC) was established. Administrative expedients exploited by the civic coalition included the private, nonprofit corporation as well as the public authority.

A report by the Pennsylvania Economy League led to the organization of the RIDC in 1955. "Industrial development activity," the League observed, "is steadily becoming more competi-

[60] Pittsburgh City Planning Commission, Department of City Planning, *Annual Report* (1962), 5; Pittsburgh City Planning Commission, Department of City Planning, *Annual Report* (1963), 5.
[61] Pittsburgh City Planning Commission, Department of City Planning, *Annual Report* (1960), 3; Department of City Planning, *Annual Report* (1963), 5–10; Pittsburgh Department of City Planning, *Plans and Progress—Pittsburgh Planning* (December 6, 1963), 2.

tive and complex, requiring a highly organized and coordinated approach both by individual communities and by regions." New firms and jobs would not "automatically distribute themselves in proportion to the present distribution of facilities and employment." On the contrary, the trend was "toward locations away from existing industrial centers."[62] A region had to mobilize for purposes of industrial promotion—deliberately exploiting its assets and minimizing or eliminating its competitive handicaps.

The RIDC reorganized in 1962, becoming a development company. It established an Industrial Development Fund to provide long-term and equity capital for firms in a nine-county region. A Development Division was empowered to acquire and improve land, including the organization of industrial packages and industrial parks. By mid-1966, the Fund exceeded $9 million in commitments to "small, growing companies." The major RIDC project was a 600-acre industrial park in O'Hara Township (Allegheny County).[63]

In seeking to improve the region's competitive position, the RIDC and its director, Robert H. Ryan, stressed the need for diversification and planning. Economic progress, Ryan argued, was "just not going to happen naturally." Diversification would not be achieved without planning and "intelligent handling."[64] The region's dependence on its traditional heavy industry mix had to be consciously modified in favor of space, electronics, and research and development enterprises.

[62] Pennsylvania Economy League, Inc., Western Division, A More Effective Industrial Development Program for the Pittsburgh Region (prepared at the request of Allegheny Conference on Community Development for the Joint Committee of the Allegheny Conference and the Pittsburgh Chamber of Commerce, November 1, 1954), 1, 11.

[63] RIDC Industrial Development Fund, Third Annual Report (1965), 3; Regional Industrial Development Corporation of Southwestern Pennsylvania, The Mid-Sixties: Profile for Future Regional Growth, Fifth Annual Report (1966), 3, 6. The nine-county region in which the RIDC operated encompassed Allegheny, Armstrong, Beaver, Butler, Fayette, Greene, Lawrence, Washington, and Westmoreland.

[64] Robert H. Ryan, "Opportunities in Industrial Development," in Southwestern Pennsylvania Regional Planning Commission, First Annual Conference, Proceedings (April 25, 1963), 23. Ryan became president of the RIDC in 1964, and resigned in 1967. On his contribution, see Pittsburgh Press, July 7, 9, 1967.

The same themes of planned intervention, diversification, and nurture of "highly scientifically oriented and highly technologically oriented" activity pervaded the *Economic Study of the Pittsburgh Region*.[65] "If we look at the Pittsburgh Region's future as being foreshadowed by past trends," study director Edgar Hoover argued, "we do not like what we see. We see a major industrial area that has lagged more and more behind the national procession for half a century—with relatively slow growth in population and employment, chronically high employment, with slow growth of new industries or other sources of jobs and income, and a swelling net outflow of people."[66] Fortunately, economic development was tied far less to the locational advantages that Pittsburgh had exploited in the nineteenth century. The region, therefore, could shape its own future, creating an environment attractive to the professional and scientific personnel upon whom future growth depended.[67]

[65] *Economic Study of the Pittsburgh Region* (conducted by the Pittsburgh Regional Planning Association), Vol. 1, *Region in Transition* (Pittsburgh: University of Pittsburgh Press, 1963); Vol. II, *Portrait of a Region* (Pittsburgh: University of Pittsburgh Press, 1963); Vol. III, *Region with a Future* (Pittsburgh: University of Pittsburgh Press, 1963).

[66] Edgar M. Hoover, "The Economic Outlook for the Region," in Southwestern Pennsylvania Regional Planning Commission, First Annual Conference, *Proceedings* (1963), 11.

[67] One of the most ambitious efforts in this direction was a complete fiasco. The Oakland Corporation was created, amid much fanfare, in March, 1962. Its chairman was Edward H. Litchfield, then Chancellor of the University of Pittsburgh, and it included the major Oakland educational institutions. The object of the Corporation was to develop the Panther Hollow ravine, situated between the Carnegie-Mellon and University of Pittsburgh campuses, into a multilevel, $250 million community of laboratories, offices, shops, theaters, parks, and transit facilities. It was described as a vision of the twenty-first century city, "a city in which the individual can find rewarding employment, recreation, culture and higher education, all within walking distance of his home." Panther Hollow was also closely tied to the aspirations for diversification, centering on R & D. "The economy of the Upper Appalachian region is oriented toward heavy industry, metals and mining. There is a growing need for diversification. . . . Research, with deliberately managed 'spin-off' of laboratory developments into new and existing regional industrial activity is about the only solution to the problem." Similarly, "we visualize the kind of environment that will attract skilled, well-educated, highly-trained and experienced people that the institutions and the businesses and the neighborhoods of Pittsburgh need. . . ." See Fred Smith, "What the

The aspiration for economic growth helps explain the Renaissance leadership's ritualistic praise of culture and environmental amenity. The Southwestern Pennsylvania Regional Planning Commission observed that "intellectual and cultural resources . . . appear to be essential to research and development employees." They demanded, among other things, "good quality housing in communities with superior school systems."[68] Similarly, Bernard Loshbough, director of ACTION-Housing, observed that industrial development today was "dependent as never before upon the employment of professional men and skilled workers, and these are the people who demand worthy living environments for themselves and for their children."[69] And, as Hoover testified, the "highly-qualified professional and technical people and business enterprises who are in demand everywhere" themselves demanded a "high standard of residential amenity and high cultural and professional opportunities."[70]

Pittsburgh did improve its status as a research and management center in the post-War period. This did not occur, however, because the city emerged as a cultural and visual Mecca. More

Oakland Corporation is All About," *Pittsburgh Business Review*, 33 (January 1963), 1–3; Oakland Corporation, *This is an Urban Area* (n.d.).

The Panther Hollow project and Oakland Corporation passed quietly into oblivion. Other proposals for environmental reconstruction, such as the new towns proposed by the Southwestern Pennsylvania Regional Planning Commission and ACTION-Housing, also seem to involve too drastic and imaginative a modification of the status quo for the CBD-oriented civic coalition. See Southwestern Pennsylvania Regional Planning Commission, *Alternative Regional Development Patterns* (August 1965); and ACTION-Housing, Inc., *The Feasibility of Residential Development in the Proposed Collier Township Renewal Area* (October 1963). The Southwestern Pennsylvania Regional Planning Commission, established in 1962, is based on the six county region defined in the *Economic Study of the Pittsburgh Region*: Allegheny, Armstrong, Beaver, Butler, Washington, and Westmoreland. It consists of three members from each of the counties, who share staff and facilities with the Pittsburgh Regional Planning Association.

[68] Southwestern Pennsylvania Regional Planning Commission, *Land for Industry: A Summary of Findings and Recommendations of the Industrial Land Study*, Regional Plan Summary Report No. 1 (June 1965), n.p.

[69] Bernard E. Loshbough, "Opportunities in Living Areas," in Southwestern Pennsylvania Regional Planning Commission, First Annual Conference, *Proceedings* (April 25, 1963), 49A.

[70] *Ibid.*, 16.

important was the fact that major corporations already had their offices and laboratories in the Pittsburgh area. The creation of the reverse welfare state encouraged further expansion among established industries and firms.

The economic achievements of the Pittsburgh Renaissance were the product of consensus on community policy; but while corporations thrive on consensus, cultural vitality has other roots. The problems of cultural growth in a corporation-dominated environment were dramatized in the demise of repertory theater in Pittsburgh. The brilliant American Conservatory Theater, under the direction of William Ball, survived only the 1965–1966 season at the hitherto low-grade Pittsburgh Playhouse; his successor, William Hancock, was summarily dismissed the following year. The Playhouse reverted back to a policy of community theater—meaning a bland, noncontroversial diet of Miller, Shaw, and Shakespeare. This, too, failed, and the Pittsburgh Playhouse was finally turned over to a local community college to mount student productions.

The Playhouse, it seemed, belonged to a Board of Directors who presumed to "set artistic standards for a professional company." Businessmen or their representatives in Pittsburgh felt "competent to set artistic policy" for the cultural enterprises they controlled. In the end, the "threatre aristocracy . . . fired two directors (Bill Ball and John Hancock) and produced no excitement and no education." In the last year of the Playhouse, all efforts by the company to "establish the repertory image were unequivocally discouraged." Apparently, this was "too 'closely associated' with the anathema of Bill Ball and John Hancock radicalism"—with a theater of "engagement" rather than "entertainment."[71]

The Pittsburgh Renaissance was an extraordinary episode in American urban development. It had no precedent in terms of mobilization of civic resources at the elite level and wholesale environmental intervention. The achievement, however, was administrative and political in character; the civic coalition was dominated by corporate and political managers. It is suggestive that the civic coalition's most dramatic failure—the Lower Hill

[71] *Pittsburgh Point,* May 30, 1968. Quotations are from Howard Witt, a member of the Pittsburgh Playhouse Company in its last year.

—was the only one that involved a major cultural program. Environmental amenity does not, any more than culture, flow inevitably from managerial prowess that can engineer large-scale physical change. Architecture and design were always secondary considerations in the Renaissance. Pittsburgh's natural endowments were not exploited fully, and imaginative improvement plans were ignored or made token progress.

A landscape architect has pointed out that the "most important single characteristic of Pittsburgh is the factor of contrast within its own political boundaries":[72] the three rivers, undulating terrain, and variety and richness of the verdure. But the river banks remain underdeveloped for recreational and scenic purposes, and "much of the Triangle has lost its visual relationship with the three rivers."[73] Numerous proposals have been made for more imaginative housing and landscaping on the steep slopes that comprise nearly 30 percent of the city's net land area. As ACTION-Housing has noted, a stranger to Pittsburgh must find it "incredible that this visual drama is so little exploited."[74] The failure is especially incredible in light of the economic drain represented by the steep slopes. Much tax delinquent property is concentrated in these areas. Their extensive blight exerts a "depressing effect on the surrounding developed areas discouraging their conservation and improvement." Finally, servicing of

[72] Patrick Horsbrugh, "Contrast in Urban Design," *Landscape Architecture,* 53 (April 1963), 196–201.
[73] David A. Wallace, *Report on Pittsburgh: A Conceptual Critique of the Oakland and Golden Triangle Areas* (at the invitation of the Pittsburgh Regional Planning Association for the Pittsburgh City Planning Commission, Golden Triangle Study Committee, Oakland Study Advisory Committee, May 1961), 29. In the tradition of Frederick Law Olmsted, Jr., see *A Master Plan for the Development of Riverfronts and Hillsides in the City of Pittsburgh,* July 1959 (prepared by Griswold, Winters, and Swain, under the direction of the Department of Parks and Recreation). There is some hope that the Stadium and other redevelopment projects along the Allegheny and Ohio Rivers on the North Side will invigorate those "forlorn urban shores." *Pittsburgh Post-Gazette,* November 23, 1967. See also, *Pittsburgh Post-Gazette,* April 6, 1968, and *Pittsburgh Press,* May 19, 1968, which describe the objectives of the newly organized Three Rivers Improvement and Development Corporation (TRIAD).
[74] ACTION-Housing, Inc., *Steep-Slope Housing: A Feasibility Report, Mount Washington, Pittsburgh* (October 1965), 1.

Slope housing: houses seen from Larimer Avenue Bridge
above Washington Boulevard, 1951.

the steep slopes in their present haphazard pattern of development is inordinately expensive and difficult.[75]

The keystone of the reverse welfare state—Golden Triangle
renewal—epitomized the managerial approach to urban environment and culture. The CBD is being transformed into an enor-
mous filling cabinet, which operates between the hours of 9–5.

[75] ACTION-Housing, Inc., *Steep-Slope Renewal: Its Opportunity and Challenge* (Urban Renewal Impact Study, September 1963), 5, 6, 12–13. Also,
Edward E. Smuts, "Steep-Slope Economics: The Pittsburgh Case," *Landscape Architecture*, 53 (April 1963), 202–205. Smuts points out that the
City of Pittsburgh consisted of 29,000 acres, exclusive of streets. Of the
9800 undeveloped acres, 8400 or 29 percent of the city's net area, consisted
of slopes of more than 15 percent grade (and most were over 25 percent).
Public control of steep slopes is advocated in William G. Swain, "Making
up for 200-Year Loss in Pittsburgh," *Landscape Architecture* 50 (Winter
1959–1960), 76–80.

The expressionless stainless-steel facades of the Gateway offices tower over grass and walks: no shops, no entertainment, no restaurants of note, no nightlife. Throughout the Golden Triangle, office buildings have, rabbit-like, generated more offices, and little else. The problem is not limited to an advanced state of functional sterility. Architectural and design opportunities have been ignored. "Within the Triangle, and immediately adjacent thereto," the Regional Planning Association has complained, "the visually strong areas of the Point State Park, Gateway Center, Mellon Square and the Civic Auditorium suffer because of their poor relationships to each other and to surrounding areas." To cope with the visual sterility, it proposed a series of public parks and squares, pedestrian walkways along Fifth Avenue and Smithfield Streets, and extensive landscaping.[76]

In the late 1960's a group of Pittsburgh architects and artists published a "manifesto" expressing their determination to no longer silently watch "our City being defaced by thoughtless buildings and projects. . . . The inane things that have all but ruined this place have been unchallenged much too long."[77] This kind of protest involved no serious challenge to the decision making prerogatives of the civic coalition. Exponents of environmental amenity possessed no political or financial leverage, and it was too late to prevent the mass atrocities already committed downtown (as well as in Oakland by Carnegie-Mellon University and the University of Pittsburgh).[78] A second, more ominous form of protest also emerged by the 1960's, associated with the

[76] Pittsburgh Regional Planning Association, *A Plan for Pittsburgh's Golden Triangle* (1962), 102, 106. To cope with the functional sterility, the Association proposed a major downtown entertainment area for the performing arts, and a second area for night clubs and specialty restaurants.

[77] *Pittsburgh Point*, April 6, 1967. The six signers were: Antoni de Chicchis, architect; James Lesko, designer; Gordon Yee, sculptor; Joe Nicholson, Chatham College Faculty; and Delbert Highlands and Troy West, architects.

[78] The authors of the statement were especially irked that Carnegie-Mellon University allowed its campus "to be raped by a little tower" (administration building) designed by a west coast architectural firm. They write off the University of Pittsburgh as hopeless now that "its building programs and policies are to be determined by the General State Authority." The criticism of Oakland's major universities was well taken. Carnegie-Mellon has favored a bland modern architectural style; the University of Pittsburgh suffers from a concrete fortress or penitentiary syndrome.

civil rights and poverty issues. It concerned slum housing, neighborhood power, and the general social implications of the reverse welfare state. In response to these new pressures, the ACCD ostensibly revised its priorities in the late 1960's. Robert Pease left the Urban Renewal Authority in January, 1968 to become director of the ACCD, now committed to a "social Renaissance." Henry L. Hillman, the Conference president, conceded that it had "failed to recognize the urban crisis" in the past, but would now concentrate upon slum improvement.[79]

[79] *Pittsburgh Post-Gazette,* June 25, 1968.

SEVEN

The Social Dimensions of the Renaissance

In the early years of the Renaissance, the director of the Pittsburgh Housing Association warned that Pittsburgh, "for all its dreams of a sterilized, streamlined city of the future, is in trouble, serious trouble. Its housing gets older and more decayed by the hour."[1] The original emphasis on renewal as an instrument of economic reconstruction led, furthermore, to a reduction in the net supply of low-cost housing. By the late 1950's the housing problem could no longer be ignored in light of shortages, extensive deterioration of the existing stock, and relocation difficulties dramatized by the Lower Hill redevelopment. Not least important, as the Allegheny Conference on Community Development was informed, "housing is no longer a mere matter of consumption, entirely detached from the sphere of industrial production; it has become a weapon in . . . inter-areal competition for industry."[2]

[1] Wilson S. Borland, "Pittsburgh's Housing: In Trouble," *Federator*, 22 (September 1947), 8. Replaced by ACTION-Housing in 1957, the Pittsburgh Housing Association had become ineffectual after World War II, "paralyzed by a divided board, a cautious executive and a narrow conception . . . of the field of action of a Chest agency." C.E.A. Winslow, "Report on the Role of a Voluntary Agency, the Extent to Which the Aims of Such an Agency are Attained in Pittsburgh, and the Methods by Which They Could be Attained" (mimeographed, 1948), in Pittsburgh Housing Association, Minutes, July 1, 1948.

[2] Max Nurnberg, *Housing Survey of Pittsburgh and Allegheny County* (Allegheny Conference on Community Development, Pittsburgh, July 1946), Part I. Factual Report. Section I, Text, 8. Also, Max Nurnberg, *Recent Trends in the Housing Market of Pittsburgh and Allegheny County* (Allegheny Conference on Community Development, June 1950). These two reports represent an exhaustive survey of Pittsburgh housing conditions in the 1940's.

Almost half the dwelling units (238,000) in Allegheny County in 1960 were built before 1920; more than 90,000 originated before 1900. The average house in older settlement areas, including Pittsburgh, was over 50 years old. The 1960 census data indicated that 112,318 dwelling units, 22.3 percent of the County total of 503,006, were "deficient" (17,444, 3.4 percent, were "dilapidated"; 67,809, 13.5 percent, were "deteriorating"; and 27,065, 5.4 percent were classified as sound but without plumbing). Most of the deficient housing, 81 percent, was concentrated in Pittsburgh and the older areas. New construction averaged only 1 percent of the housing inventory each year. Only 13 of 80 municipalities with extensive blight problems had a renewal program in progress or in the planning stage.[3] The situation, a Pittsburgh newspaper conceded, was "frankly, frightening in the dimensions of the deteriorated conditions."[4]

Deficiences in governmental organization impeded both the "development of new housing and the improvement of existing housing." Some kind of municipal or regional planning commission encompassed 71 percent of the County land area and 81 percent of its population, but only Allegheny County and Pittsburgh maintained "staffs capable of carrying on a comprehensive planning program, including the preparation of a master plan." Most communities, 92 or 72.4 percent, had zoning ordinances; these

[3] ACTION-Housing, *Urban Renewal Impact Study: Summary* (June 1963), 15, 16; ACTION-Housing, *Urban Renewal Impact Study: The General Report* (October 1963), 16. Dilapidated housing was defined as housing that "does not provide safe and adequate shelter. It has one or more critical defects; or has a combination of intermediate defects; or is of inadequate original construction." Deteriorating housing "needs more repair than would be provided in the course of regular maintenance. It has one or more defects of an intermediate nature that must be corrected if the unit is to continue to provide safe and adequate shelter. Examples of such defects are shaky or unsafe porch or steps; broken plaster; rotten window sills or frames. Such defects are of neglect which lead to serious structural damage if not corrected." (*Ibid.*, 16, 15.)

Other volumes in the Urban Renewal Impact Study, prepared by ACTION-Housing, include: *Steep-Slope Renewal-Opportunity* (September 1963); *Coordinating Urban Renewal and Highway Planning and Development.* The volume, *Administrative-Legal-Fiscal*, was prepared by the Pennsylvania Economy League, Western Division, for ACTION-Housing.
[4] *Pittsburgh Press*, June 27, 1963.

affected 80 percent of the County land area and 93 percent of the population, but "in most cases the enforcement officer was a part-time employee or carried out this function in addition to other municipal duties." Fewer communities, 53, had adopted sub-division controls. Building codes existed in 82 communities, 65 percent, but many had been enacted to qualify for federal renewal assistance, and "little or no consideration is given to effectively administering and enforcing the regulations adopted."[5]

Thus numerous communities lacked planning, subdivision, zoning, and building controls, or adequate provision for their enforcement. Equally important, these regulatory mechanisms were not only incapable of producing new housing, but often served to obstruct development because of their lack of uniformity or their use to control the influx of population. Suburban municipalities imposed "stringent restrictions" for fear that additional "home owners will outpace their town's ability to provide schools and other facilities. These restrictions . . . call for minimum lot sizes and frontages which make it economically impossible to build housing in the moderate income bracket."[6]

A Pennsylvania Economy League report, sponsored by the ACCD and published in 1957, explicitly linked the future of the renewal program with a resolution of the housing deadlock. "While considerable housing is being constructed, the minority, aged, and lower-middle-income housing market has been neglected even though it is this class of residential property which is sorely needed for relocating the families which must be moved as a result of redevelopment projects and the application of minimum housing standards."[7] In order to assist a population and

[5] *Allegheny Council to Improve Our Neighborhoods-Housing: An Action Program for Meeting the Housing Problems of Allegheny County,* February 1957 (prepared for Allegheny Conference on Community Development by Pennsylvania Economy League, Inc.—Western Division), 30; ACTION-Housing, *Urban Renewal Impact Study: Administrative-Legal-Fiscal,* 26, 34, 47, 52, 54, 59, 66.

[6] *An Action Program for Meeting the Housing Problems of Allegheny County,* 36.

[7] *Ibid.,* "Summary of Findings and Conclusions." Similarly, "the Allegheny Conference on Community Development knew that expansion of the renewal program in the County would mean displacing additional thousands of families in the next few years. Relocation housing was practically non-

income bracket "above the public housing level" but unable to acquire new housing in the private market, the League recommended the establishment of a voluntary, nonprofit agency—the Allegheny Council to Improve Our Neighborhoods-Housing (ACTION-Housing, Inc.). Established in 1957, ACTION-Housing focused upon "moderate income families," which it defined as the 43 percent of county families in the income range of $5000–9000.[8]

Under executive director Bernard E. Loshbough, ACTION-Housing during its first decade developed a program that encompassed the sponsorship of new and rehabilitated housing, neighborhood citizen organization, and research.[9] The agency possessed three distinctive characteristics. Although nonprofit, it was also briskly businesslike in its operations. Far removed from the realm of amateur humanitarianism, its administrative, research, and public relations methods resembled those of the corporation. Loshbough was especially proficient in the translation of ideas into operating programs, including the arrangement of housing or community organization packages. ACTION-Housing, in essence, embodied the application of managerial and professional expertise to housing betterment and neighborhood intervention.

Along with the no-nonsense, corporate flair that pervaded its operations, ACTION-Housing pioneered in efforts to mobilize

existent. This shortage could easily develop into a major roadblock. . . ." Theodore H. Savage, "ACTION-Housing," *Greater Pittsburgh,* 39 (December 1957), 15.

[8] Bernard E. Loshbough, *The County's Housing Needs—An Overview* (ACTION-Housing News Release, September 26, 1966), 6. "To serve these families," Loshbough specified, "means producing new housing at between $12,000 and $15,000, and rehabilitated housing at $10,000 or less, at a monthly charge that the moderate income family can afford."

[9] Loshbough holds a degree in architecture from the University of Notre Dame. Before coming to Pittsburgh, he served as General Manager of the National Housing Center (National Association of Home Builders), Washington, D.C. Previous to that, he spent three years in India as Deputy Representative of the Ford Foundation, and another year working for the Department of State. Earlier positions included Director, Housing and Community Facilities Division, Executive Office of the President, National Security Resources Board, Washington, D.C.; Administrator of Connecticut state housing programs; and Deputy-in-charge of Operations, National Capital Housing Authority.

private funds to achieve public purposes. It thus anticipated the national interest that developed by the late 1960's in providing incentives to corporations to deal with such problems as unemployment and slum housing. At the same time, ACTION-Housing was quick, in the tradition of the Pittsburgh Renaissance, to exploit all available forms of governmental assistance.

As its efforts to link the public and private sectors suggest, ACTION-Housing favored an experimental approach to housing and neighborhood development. It was, however, a disciplined experimentation, based always on painstaking exploratory research and economic feasibility. Well-versed in the intricacies of housing financing, Loshbough stressed that "people may want a certain kind of housing, depending upon their needs and desire, but the kind of housing people get is heavily dependent upon economics."[10] Equally important, ACTION-Housing favored experimental or demonstration programs that could be duplicated in Pittsburgh and elsewhere.

In seeking support for its operations (particularly those dependent upon private investment), ACTION-Housing benefited from a distinguished roster of sponsors and directors.[11] J. Stanley Purnell, Assistant to the President of T. Mellon and Sons, served as chairman of the Board and, for a time, President of ACTION-Housing. Purnell was instrumental in the creation of the vitally important Development Fund in 1959. Some mechanism through which to acquire sites and supply intermediate equity or seed capital to builders had taken "priority as a major need almost from the beginning. The question was, how best to raise the money, and to manage this equity capital in a sound, businesslike manner."[12] After extensive investigation, ACTION-Housing de-

---

[10] Bernard E. Loshbough, *Good Housing for All of Our People* (Address, Conference of National Organizations, April 29, 1966) (ACTION-Housing, News Release), 2.

[11] In 1967 the ACTION-Housing Board of Directors included Richard K. Mellon; Frank E. Agnew, Jr., Chairman of the Board, Pittsburgh National Bank; Donald C. Burnham, President, Westinghouse Electric Corporation; M. A. Cancelliere, President, Western Pennsylvania National Bank; H. J. Heinz II; and Alfred M. Hunt, Vice President and Secretary, Aluminum Company of America.

[12] J. Stanley Purnell, *Financing the Corporation. The Pittsburgh Experience: Loans and Grants* (Address, National Conference on Development Funds

cided to establish a revolving development fund.[13] Purnell presented the proposal to three Mellon foundations: Sarah Mellon
Scaife, Richard King Mellon, and A. W. Mellon Educational and
Charitable Trust. They responded with grants totaling $350,000,
which served as "front money" in the subscription drive. Purnell
then contacted top officials of Westinghouse Electric, Jones and
Laughlin, and U.S. Steel—the largest corporate employers in the
Pittsburgh area. The presidents of these companies expressed a
"strong interest" in the proposal in the summer of 1959, and in the
following months Purnell met with "high officials" of other
corporations. Established in 1959, the Development Fund totaled
over $1,500,000 after two years (more than $1 million in interest-
bearing loan subscriptions and the balance in grants).[14] The
loan subscriptions ranged from $10,000 to $250,000; beginning in
1963 the Development Fund began annual payment of promised
4 percent dividends.[15] The emphasis upon dividends and the

and Nonprofit Housing Development Corporations, November 20, 1967)
(ACTION-Housing, News Release), 1.

[13] A Development Fund had been established in Cleveland in 1954 "as a
charitable foundation to aid the civic and governmental agencies to get
under way a practical urban renewal program." It raised a $2 million re-
volving fund. Other precedents included the Citizens Redevelopment Corporation, established in Detroit in 1954, and the Baltimore Fight-Blight
Fund. See *An Action Program for Meeting the Housing Problems of
Allegheny County*, 46 ff; *Pittsburgh Development Fund of ACTION-Housing: A Proposal* (July 1959).

[14] Bernard E. Loshbough, *The Role of a Non-Profit Corporation* (ACTION-
Housing, News Release, April 18, 1961), 2, 3; Purnell, *Financing the
Corporation*, 1-2. The Development Fund is managed by a Finance Committee selected by ACTION-Housing's Board of Directors. The original goal
had been to raise $2 million, but it was decided that $1,580,000 was sufficient.

[15] A recent list of grantors and subscribers to the Pittsburgh Development
Fund, prepared by ACTION-Housing, includes the following companies.

The Alcoa Foundation
Allegheny Ludlum Steel Corporation
Columbia Gas of Pennsylvania, Inc.
Commonwealth Trust Company
Consolidation Coal Company
Crane Company
Duquesne Gas Company
Equitable Gas Company

Gulf Oil Corporation
Jones & Laughlin Steel Corporation
Koppers Company, Inc.
The Levinson Steel Company
Mellon National Bank and Trust
    Company
The A. W. Mellon Educational and
    Charitable Trust

deliberate encouragement of loans rather than grants were typical of ACTION-Housing's determination to make its operations as "businesslike as possible."[16]

The establishment of the Development Fund had been preceded by an experiment in moderate rental housing. Spring Hill Gardens, opened in 1959, consisted of 209 apartment units on the North Side. It was sponsored by ACTION-Housing through a nonprofit corporation, and financed by 100 percent FHA mortgage insurance under Section 221 of the National Housing Act.[17] A leading objective was to demonstrate that with "careful selection of tenants, able management, and an equitable occupancy pattern, moderate integration is no bar to the successful operation of a rental development."[18] In other words, racial balance, through use of the quota system, was commercially and socially feasible.

Planning began in 1959 for East Hills Park, a major undertaking involving use of the Development Fund.[19] ACTION-Housing

Mine Safety Appliances Company	Sarah Mellon Scaife Foundation
The Peoples Natural Gas Company	The Union National Bank of Pittsburgh
Pittsburgh Coke & Chemical Company	
	United States Steel Corporation
Pittsburgh National Bank	West Penn Power Company
The Pittsburgh Plate Glass Foundation	Western Pennsylvania National Bank
	Westinghouse Air Brake Company
Retail Merchants Association	Westinghouse Electric Corporation
Rockwell Manufacturing Company	Edwin L. Wiegand Company

[16] The relationship between the Development Fund and builders was equally businesslike. "The Development Fund makes short-term loans to developers at the prevailing rate of interest. The differential between this rate and the interest due subscribers is used to meet the administrative cost of the Fund. In order to turn money over rapidly and maintain the revolving loan feature of the Fund, the term of loans to developers is not to exceed five years. . . ." The Fund also supplies a range of important services that benefit the developer: preliminary architectural and site-planning studies; marketing aid; liaison with government and unions. See ACTION-Housing, *The Pittsburgh Development Fund of ACTION-Housing, Inc.* (n.d.), *passim*.

[17] Unless otherwise noted, data on ACTION-Housing's new and rehabilitated housing is drawn from its semi-annual reports.

[18] ACTION-Housing (Executive Director's) *Report to the Board of Directors and Members,* September 1960, 6. In 1965 Spring Hill Gardens was sold to the G. L. Marhoefer Realty Company.

[19] The contract with the developer allowed ACTION-Housing to exercise

hoped to provide a large-scale *"demonstration of new techniques in housing design, production and site layout."* This depended, in turn, upon a "moratorium on past restrictions: architects, building materials producers, and labor must be allowed to innovate with only the restraints of their professional integrity."[20] ACTION-Housing acquired a vacant 130-acre site on the eastern edge of Pittsburgh. Construction began in 1961 on Phase I of a projected 1000–1400 dwelling units. Within three years, 187 FHA-insured townhouses had been erected on land sold by ACTION-Housing to the private builder, Catranel, Inc. Late in 1966 the final section of Phase I—91 apartments in eight 3-story buildings—was begun. In contrast to the townhouses (an FHA section 203b sales project), these were limited-dividend, rental units.

The FHA approved a $5 million mortgage commitment for Phase II of East Hills in September, 1967. This involved the construction of 196 apartments in low-rise (four story) clusters, and 130 townhouses in quadri-plex design (four units joined from a central core). The Phase II sponsor was Housing Equities, an ACTION-Housing affiliate. Financing was based upon section 221d3 of the National Housing Act. Enacted in 1961, amended in 1965, 221d3 was designed to encourage the construction of moderate income housing; it enabled certain kinds of sponsors—nonprofit, limited dividend, and cooperative—to obtain mortgage funds at below-market interest rates.

East Hills Park exemplified ACTION-Housing's managerial proficiency, experimentalism, and early emphasis on utilization of public and private funds. The agency had served as promoter-entrepreneur for a complex housing package whose innovations extended to subdivision planning as well as financing. The townhouse cluster arrangement was made possible by an amendment to the Pittsburgh zoning code in 1961, authorizing "planned

---

close supervision over all building and site plans. ACTION-Housing, on the other hand, "assumed responsibility for aiding the developer in obtaining necessary zoning changes, in FHA processing, in matters involving building code changes, and in arranging for construction and permanent financing." ACTION-Housing, *The Pittsburgh Development Fund. . .* , 8.
[20] *Report on Action to Achieve Potentials for Housing in the Pittsburgh Area* (prepared for ACTION-Housing, Inc. by ACTION Research Committee, American Council to Improve Our Neighborhoods) (New York, 1959), 3, 4.

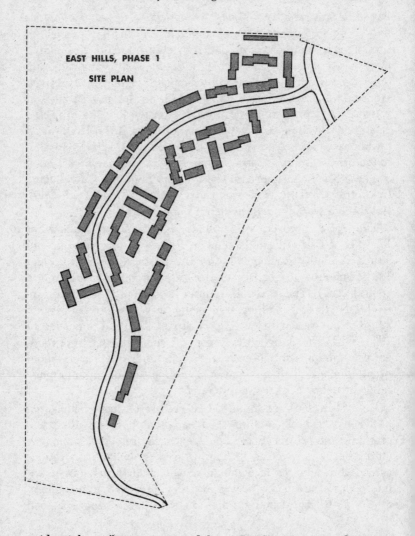

EAST HILLS, PHASE 1

SITE PLAN

residential unit" zoning; urged by ACTION-Housing, this permitted greater flexibility in land uses. Cluster housing, in turn,
had significant economic and design implications, as at Chatham
Village. It enabled planners to group open space in the form of
central courts, and led to reductions in utility and road costs.
ACTION-Housing estimated that the cluster arrangement reduced the average cost per dwelling unit for site work by 40
percent.

East Hills.

East Hills Park also benefited from special labor union concessions. The Building and Construction Trades Council signed an unusual contract with the East Hills developer in the spring of 1961. It enabled the builder and his subcontractors to use any equipment or construction techniques, prohibited jurisdictional disputes, reduced the wage scale 10 percent below that for ordinary commercial construction (except for apartment buildings), allowed the builder to hire his own labor if his request for workers was not filled within 72 hours by the Trades Council, and provided regular wages for Saturday work which substituted for days lost because of bad weather. In addition, union pension funds were made available for loans to home buyers on liberal terms.[21] These special arrangements and the economies of scale enabled ACTION-Housing to sell homes at prices considerably below those for comparable accommodations in the private market.[22]

ACTION-Housing had launched a second Development Fund enterprise in 1963. Sheraden Park, a 188-unit townhouse coopera-

[21] The union pension funds made possible 35 year mortgages at 4¾ percent interest.

[22] Prices for the East Hills Park townhouses in the mid-1960's ranged from $12,350 for a 2-bedroom unit to a high of $18,995 for a duplex model. The builder for Phase I was Roland S. Catarinella, president of Catranel, Inc. The principal architect was B. Kenneth Johnstone. Landscape architects and site engineers were Simonds and Simonds. Satterlee and Smith of Washington, D.C. served as consulting architects.

East Hills.

tive, was located in the West End of Pittsburgh.[23] Sheraden Park
was significant in suggesting a new formula for constructing
housing on city-owned land. The site had been held by the City
of Pittsburgh for tax delinquency. The land was conveyed to the
Urban Redevelopment Authority upon payment through the
ACTION-Housing Development Fund of $15,832 in back taxes.
The URA then leased the property to ACTION-Housing for
$1 a year for 55 years; ACTION-Housing, in turn, leased the
land to the developer. The Pittsburgh Department of Parks
acquired additional acreage surrounding Sheraden Park on three
sides.[24] Favorable financing terms were arranged with the FHA
under section 221d3. The housing was sold for 20 percent less
than comparable accommodations built under conventional
auspices. Monthly costs, including utilities and maintenance,
ranged from $107 (2-bedroom) to $140 (4-bedroom). Average
family income of residents in 1967 totaled $5878; the two largest
occupational categories were clerk (52 family heads) and factory-
steel mill worker (44 family heads).[25]

ACTION-Housing, during its first decade, sponsored over $13
million worth of new housing: Spring Hill Gardens, $1,776,500;

[23] As at East Hills, special arrangements were made with the Building
Trades Council, and the City of Pittsburgh agreed to rezone the area to
"planned residential unit" in order to permit cluster subdivision.

[24] ACTION-Housing, *News Bulletin*, August 11, 1965.

[25] ACTION-Housing, *Sheraden Park—188 Townhouses. Final Breakdown of
187 Sales—August 31, 1967* (data sheet).

Sheraden Park, $2,750,000; East Hills Park, Phase I, $3,700,000, and Phase II, an estimated $5,062,000. Including the projected 326 units of Phase II, the new housing in Pittsburgh was increased by 1001 moderate-income units.[26] At the same time, ACTION-Housing had always been interested in an alternative rehabilitation strategy. This interest intensified toward the late 1960's, when rehabilitation schemes overshadowed new construction in ACTION-Housing's long-range planning. The rehabilitation conception was broad, involving social as well as physical objectives. ACTION-Housing maintained that this "vital element in the urban renewal process" was not only a "powerful deterrent against blight and slums, but also a practical method of strengthening and preserving the social and economic values inherent in our older, but still sound neighborhoods."[27]

The agency in 1960 proclaimed the unfolding of a "new chapter in the Pittsburgh Renaissance story." The Amber Lumber and Supply Company, in cooperation with ACTION-Housing and *Life Magazine*, launched a home modernization demonstration at 7657 Baxter Street in Homewood-Brushton. The 10,000 persons who visited the remodeled 57-year-old house "saw the kinds of home improvements available through a lumber dealer, and how a house could be modernized on a room-by-room basis."[28] The

[26] ACTION-Housing, *New and Rehabilitated Housing Sponsored by ACTION-Housing, Inc.*, December 12, 1967 (data sheet). Early in 1968, another housing development was at the advanced planning stage. ACTION-Housing anticipated using the Development Fund in connection with the $4,800,000 "Liberty Park," Phase I, in the East Liberty renewal area. According to the plans, Liberty Park would total approximately 332 dwelling units (102 townhouses, 72 garden apartments, and 158 units in a 20-story apartment house). At a less advanced planning stage (in association with the City Planning Department and Urban Redevelopment Authority) was ACTION-Housing participation in "Greenway Park," Phase I, located in the West End. Five hundred dwelling units were projected at a cost of $5,500,000. Also under consideration in the spring of 1968 were Phases III and IV of East Hills, totaling 320 and 250 units, respectively. See ACTION-Housing, (President's) *Annual Report to the Board of Directors*, January, 1968; "Statement by J. Stanley Purnell, County Commissioners' Meeting with Housing Agencies," April 29, 1968.

[27] ACTION-Housing, *Proceedings of Conference on Modernization of Houses and Neighborhoods*, April 5, 1960, i.

[28] ACTION-Housing (Executive Director's) *Report to Directors and Mem-*

practical results, however, were disappointing; few orders were received by the Amber Company's newly established home modernization division. Equally unsuccessful was the 3-year effort to rehabilitate 59 houses on Wandless Street in the Upper Hill. ACTION-Housing had worked with the owner (who employed an architect and planner to develop a schematic renovation), and with the tenants who formed a self-help group. Long-term mortgage commitments could not be obtained, however, because of general neighborhood conditions and the absence of a master plan for the area. The condition of the property deteriorated, meanwhile, and by 1962 it became "economically impossible to rehabilitate the 59 houses."[29]

The Economic Opportunity Act of 1964 enabled ACTION-Housing to expand its rehabilitation efforts. The Mayor's Committee on Human Resources was established in Pittsburgh as the coordinating agency for the Community Action Program in eight "target neighborhoods." ACTION-Housing signed a contract with the Mayor's Committee to develop a self-help home improvement program, "designed to upgrade houses of low-income families in all eight economic opportunity areas."[30] The pilot program was launched in Wooster Street (5th ward) and Linton Street (3rd ward), both in the Hill District. ACTION-Housing organized classes in home improvement conducted by "indigenous" craftsmen and provided supplies. In 1966 the program was extended to other neighborhoods.

Section 221d3 of the 1965 Housing Act, which authorized

bers, September 1960, 7; ACTION-Housing (Executive Director's) *Report to the Board of Directors*, September 1961, 13.

Prior to the Baxter Street project, ACTION-Housing had sponsored the rehabilitation of a house in the Beltzhoover district.

[29] ACTION-Housing (Executive Director's) *Report to the Board of Directors*, September 11, 1962, 18.

[30] ACTION-Housing (Executive Director's) *Report to the Board of Directors*, September 1964-September 1965, 21.

The eight economic opportunity areas in Pittsburgh included the Hill District, North Side, East Liberty-Garfield, Homewood-Brushton, Southwest Pittsburgh, South Oakland, Lawrenceville, and Hazelwood-Glenwood. Elements of the city's antipoverty program, formulated by ACTION-Housing, included urban extension-community action programs in Homewood-Brushton, Hazelwood-Glenwood, South Oakland, and Lawrenceville; the self-help home improvement program; and neighborhood employment centers.

below-market interest mortgage money (3 percent) for nonprofit sponsors of rehabilitated housing approved by the FHA, provided the economic basis for a more extensive rehabilitation program. On August 1, 1966 ACTION-Housing announced the acquisition of 22 single-family houses on both sides of a Cora Street block in Homewood-Brushton. These were 60-year-old, row, two-story brick dwellings. The acquisition cost of $87,000 was met through the Development Fund; total development costs came to $259,686. Rents and utilities before rehabilitation averaged $85–90; the vastly improved rehabilitated units, completed early in 1967, rented for $86.00 to $93.50 including utilities (except electricity). Cora Street's potentialities, according to Loshbough, were "enormous." The project could lead to the opening of a "vast, virtually untapped market for the rehabilitation of older housing" and the creation of a major new industry in Pittsburgh and the nation. ACTION-Housing announced that the "large-scale private enterprise rehabilitation of old but structurally sound housing is now, and will be in the future, engaging much of the attention of ACTION-Housing."[31]

ACTION-Housing organized a conference in January, 1967 at the exclusive Duquesne Club where it formally proposed the establishment of a rehabilitation corporation. The guest list was "escalated" at a second conference in June. Participants included Richard King Mellon, Pennsylvania Governor Shafer, Senators Scott, Clark, and Percy, and top executives from Westinghouse, U.S. Steel, Alcoa, and other corporations.[32] In seeking support for the rehabilitation program, ACTION-Housing stressed the economic as well as the civic possibilities. "Can it be," J. Stanley Purnell asked, "that we, a nation of builders, have not yet learned

---

[31] ACTION-Housing, *News Bulletin* (August 1, 1966), 4; ACTION-Housing (President's) *Report to the Board of Directors,* January 1967, 2.

[32] *Pittsburgh Point,* July 6, 1967. A documentary film on Cora Street was shown at the dinner, whose formal hosts were the presidents of seven major Pittsburgh corporations: Aluminum Company of America; Duquesne Light Company; Koppers Company; Peoples Natural Gas Company; PPG Industries; United States Steel Corporation; and Westinghouse Electric Corporation. ACTION-Housing, *Statement by J Stanley Purnell, Chairman of the Board and President ACTION-Housing, Inc. before the Housing and Urban Affairs Subcommittee of the U.S. Senate Banking and Currency Committee,* Washington, D.C., July 27, 1967, 2.

Cora Street Rehabilitation (ACTION-Housing).

the economics of rebuilding? Or how to develop and adapt space-age construction systems and technologies to housing rehabilitation?" Here was the opportunity for "private enterprise to take the lead," demonstrating "what it can achieve through the appropriate application of its capabilities in an area of broad public concern." But the profit opportunities should not be minimized. "To be perfectly pragmatic, in the long run this motivation offers the most potent stimulant for action on a massive scale. After all, our profit-motivated system has proven itself to be the most prolific provider for human needs and wants yet known to man."[33]

Conceived as an experiment that combined profit and business leadership in "improving the quality of our community life," a housing rehabilitation corporation had two exceptional strategic

[33] ACTION-Housing, *Proposal for the Creation of the Allegheny Housing Rehabilitation Corporation* (June 1967), 6, 7.

Cora Street Rehabilitation (ACTION-Housing).

advantages. It attacked ghetto unemployment as well as sub-standard housing; and it satisfied the criteria for business involvement in "workable programs that have specific, limited, realistic objectives and that will show early, visible results."[34]

Following the June, 1967 conference, Purnell and Loshbough contacted the "top management" of the 40-odd companies represented.[35] In January, 1968 executives from 32 corporations, mostly Pittsburgh-based, ratified the articles of incorporation for the Allegheny Housing Rehabilitation Corporation (AHRCO). It anticipated a capitalization of $3–4 million and a production rate of 1000 rehabilitated units a year by the fifth year of operation. Completed units might be sold to nonprofit organizations, individuals, and public housing agencies, or retained by AHRCO for investment purposes.[36] A distinctive feature in the manage-

[34] Robert E. Seymour, *America's Greatest Undeveloped Market* (Address, American Marketing Association, 14th Annual Public Utilities Marketing Seminar, May 2, 3, 1968) (ACTION-Housing, reprint), 10. Seymour was president of the Peoples Natural Gas Company, Pittsburgh. Along similar lines, see Robinson F. Barker, *America's Urban Dilemma—Industry's Response to the Challenge* (Address, National Industrial Conference Board, New York, January 10, 1968) (reprint).

[35] Purnell, *Statement, Housing and Urban Affairs Subcommittee*, 6.

[36] ACTION-Housing, *News Bulletin*, January 25, 1968. AHRCO will have its own professional staff, but ACTION-Housing will be retained as a con-

ment of AHRCO was the creation of an executive committee of nineteen, including "six members representing the community interest."[37]

AHRCO launched operations quickly. In January, 1968 ACTION-Housing announced the purchase of another 78 dwell-

---

sultant. A supplementary proposal by ACTION-Housing was for the creation of a National Research Council for Housing Rehabilitation to "organize and supervise research programs with the purpose of providing necessary technical information and methodology. . . ." ACTION-Housing, *A Statement of Purpose for the Proposed National Research Council for Housing Rehabilitation* (*NHCHR*), June 20, 1967.

[37] ACTION-Housing, *News Bulletin*, April 16, 1968, 4. Members of the executive committee representing the "community interest" included Byrd R. Brown (president, Pittsburgh chapter, NAACP); Ronald R. Davenport (president, Urban League of Pittsburgh); and Dorothy Richardson (president, Citizens Against Slum Housing).

By the spring of 1968, AHRCO had acquired commitments totalling more than $2.5 million from 39 corporations and foundations:

1. Allegheny Airlines
2. Allegheny Ludlum Steel Corporation
3. Aluminum Company of America
4. Bell Telephone Company of Pennsylvania
5. Blaw-Knox Company
6. Columbia Gas of Pennsylvania, Inc.
7. Consolidation Coal Company
8. Crane Company
9. Crucible Steel Company
10. Cyclops Corporation
11. Dravo Corporation
12. Duquesne Light Company
13. Equitable Gas Company
14. The Equitable Life Assurance Society of the United States
15. Gimbel Brothers
16. Gulf Oil Corporation
17. Hahn Furniture Company
18. Harbison-Walker Refractories Company
19. H. J. Heinz Company
20. The Hillman Foundation, Inc.
21. Joseph Horne Company
22. Jones & Laughlin Steel Corporation
23. Kaufmann's Department Store
24. Ketchum, MacLeod & Grove, Inc.
25. Koppers Company, Inc.
26. Levinson Steel Company
27. Limbach Company
28. Mesta Machine Company
29. Mine Safety Appliances Company
30. National Steel Corporation
31. North American Rockwell Corporation
32. PPG Industries
33. Peoples Natural Gas Company
34. Pittsburgh Steel Company
35. Rockwell Manufacturing Company
36. Sears, Roebuck and Company (Pittsburgh)
37. United States Steel Corporation
38. Westinghouse Air Brake Company
39. Westinghouse Electric Corporation

ings spread over six streets in Homewood-Brushton.[38] The rehabilitation of 66 of these units was designated as the first
AHRCO project, and work began in April. Nine of the eleven
major subcontractors for the $816,000 "Kelly-Hamilton" project
were Negroes, signifying AHRCO's intention to expand employment opportunities for ghetto residents. Kelly-Hamilton also
marked the first combination in Pittsburgh of section 221d3 housing and rent supplements. Rent supplements applied to 24 of the
66 units and benefited families that satisfied the size and income
requirements for public housing ($4,000–4,800 gross annual in-
come). Ownership and management of the project was trans-
ferred to a nonprofit neighborhood group organized by the
Homewood Holy Cross Episcopal Church.[39]

The new and rehabilitated housing sponsored by ACTION-
Housing during its first decade represented virtually the entire
addition to the moderate-income housing stock in Pittsburgh (as
defined by FHA regulations under section 221d3, moderate in-
comes ranged from $5600 for one person to $10,400 for seven or
more in the Pittsburgh market area). In 1962 and 1963, for example, only 20 single-family housing starts were recorded for the
City of Pittsburgh in the East Hills or Sheraden Park price range.
The demonstration value of the housing was perhaps even more
significant than the quantity. ACTION-Housing, as suggested
previously, combined managerial-technical expertise, a pioneering emphasis upon the use of private as well as public funds to
achieve social goals, and an experimental approach toward all
phases of housing development. Its innovations in housing design
and finance, tempered by considerations of economic feasibility,
were numerous.

ACTION-Housing perfected use of the revolving development
fund in the sponsorship of moderate-income rehabilitated and
new housing: rentals, sales, and cooperative. On the other hand,

---

[38] *Pittsburgh Press*, January 9, 1968.
[39] ACTION-Housing, *News Bulletin*, April 16, 1968, 1–2; Bernard E. Losh-
bough, "Group Rehabilitating Homes," *American Banker*, 133 (May 29,
1968), reprint, 3; *Pittsburgh Point*, July 11, 1968. By the summer of 1968,
AHRCO was considering acquisition of an additional 144 dwelling units in
Homewood-Brushton, and 100 in East Liberty and the North Side. See
ACTION-Housing, "Allegheny Housing Rehabilitation Corporation," *News
Release*, August, 1, 1968.

it frequently demonstrated how nonprofit agencies could use the various federal housing insurance and subsidy programs, particularly section 221d3. East Hills and Sheraden Park, like Chatham Village earlier, dramatized the economic and design advantages of large-scale, cluster subdivision based upon flexible "planned residential unit" zoning. The arrangements between ACTION-Housing and several municipal agencies in the construction of Sheraden Park suggested a new strategy of public-private cooperation in the use of city-owned land. Finally, the organization of AHRCO represented a pioneering effort to develop a mechanism for large-scale housing rehabilitation.

ACTION-Housing, it should be emphasized, had not been established to provide housing for the lowest-income population (below $5000). Yet the director of the City Planning Commission pointed out in 1966 that 22,000 of the 40,500 substandard dwellings in Pittsburgh were occupied by families with incomes below $4000 a year.[40] Pittsburgh in 1960 ranked worst among the 14 largest cities in the percentage of nonwhite-occupied housing units that were classified as deteriorating or dilapidated (49.1 percent). The addition of units classified as sound but without full plumbing raised the total to 58.9 percent.[41] Loshbough, fully aware of this problem, emphasized that until the rent supplement legislation of 1965 no subsidy program existed that would enable ACTION-Housing to reach low-income population.[42]

Urban renewal, and the reaction that it had generated by the late 1950's, help explain ACTION-Housing's initial involvement in community organization. The Lower Hill redevelopment crystallized resentment against renewal projects that displaced large numbers of low-income families without providing alternative housing. Such protest was reinforced and strengthened by the civil rights movement. Social factors in renewal, including some measure of citizen participation in planning, could no longer be entirely ignored. In February, 1958 the executive committee of ACTION-Housing authorized its director to "take the necessary

[40] *Pittsburgh Point*, July 6, 1967.
[41] *Report of the National Advisory Commission on Civil Disorders* (New York: Bantam Books, 1968), 468; *Pittsburgh Post-Gazette*, March 18, 19, 20, 1968.
[42] Interview with Bernard Loshbough, June 1968.

steps leading to the organization of citizens neighborhood councils or associations in specific areas marked for urban renewal activities."[43] ACTION-Housing participated in the organization of the East Liberty Citizens Renewal Council in 1958, followed in 1959 by the Bluff Area Citizens Renewal Council.[44] Around the same time, it helped organize a McKeesport Council, the first outside the City, and advised the Perry Hilltop Citizens Action Committee in Pittsburgh's North Side. In the early 1960's, the agency worked intensively with the South Side Chamber of Commerce in connection with citizen organization for renewal.

Further impetus to citizen participation and neighborhood organization came from the City Planning Department's Community Renewal Program, launched in 1961. The next year a Social Planning Advisory Committee was established under the auspices of the CRP, and a number of social workers were employed. Under "Senior Social Planner" Morton Coleman, the CRP led to the division of the city into five area planning committees composed of representatives of local organizations. The latter were encouraged to present proposals to the area committees and City Planning Department.[45] Coleman subsequently joined Mayor Joseph Barr's executive staff, and played an important liaison role between the Mayor's office and the proliferating citizens groups generated by the CRP, urban renewal, the civil rights and antipoverty movements, and ACTION-Housing.

Although ACTION-Housing's early community organization

[43] ACTION-Housing (Executive Director's) *Report to the Board of Directors and Members*, September, 1960, 9.

[44] The East Liberty Citizens Renewal Council was the first of its kind in Pittsburgh. Dominated by neighborhood business and institutional interests, it was not a "grass roots" organization. ACTION-Housing also worked, in a minor way, with the Greater Braddock Chamber of Commerce.

[45] On the Community Renewal Program, see Pittsburgh, Department of City Planning, Community Renewal Program, Social Planning Advisory Committee, *Citizen Participation Report: Relationship to Urban Renewal and Planning*, 1964; Pittsburgh, Department of City Planning, *Evaluation of Community Organization Activities as Part of the Community Renewal Program*, 1965; Pittsburgh, Department of City Planning, Community Renewal Program, *A Report on Social Problems in Urban Renewal*, 1965.

Besides stimulating citizen organization in renewal, the CRP was of value in collecting data that aided in the development of the antipoverty and model cities programs in Pittsburgh (Morton Coleman to author).

work was closely tied to the formal urban renewal program, Loshbough always visualized a more comprehensive form of neighborhood intervention. He had lived in India for four years beginning in 1951, working for the State Department on Point 4
and with the Ford Foundation. In India he acquired his "first
exposure to the techniques and concepts of agricultural extension," notably the "use of extension techniques . . . in terms of
human motivation and communication." It occurred to Loshbough that "we could use some extension techniques and concepts in urban areas."[46] He employed James V. Cunningham as
associate director to aid in the formulation of a neighborhood
program that went beyond citizens councils in renewal and
housing rehabilitation.

Cunningham had been executive director of Chicago's Hyde
Park-Kenwood Community Conference since 1956. This widely
publicized experiment in the organization of citizens to arrest
deterioration of a neighborhood had convinced him of two
things: (1) that it was possible to renew a neighborhood without
bulldozing it—conservation and rehabilitation were alternative
and superior strategies; (2) that renewal was a long-term continuous process, whose success depended upon the establishment
of machinery for widespread citizen participation in decision
making.[47]

If Cunningham brought to Pittsburgh an alternative conception of renewal, he also introduced into the ACTION-Housing
program a certain attitude toward the role of neighborhoods in

[46] ACTION-Housing, *Urban Extension* (proceedings of the Pittsburgh Urban
Extension Conference held July 5–6, 1961, Pittsburgh, Pennsylvania), 4.
Loshbough had "worked with Dr. Douglas Ensminger in the widespread
use of these concepts in India's National Program of Community Develop-
ment, and the Government's small industries program initiated in 1954."
ACTION-Housing, *Application for a Grant from the Ford Foundation for a
Test Demonstration of Urban Extension to be Carried Out in Four Neigh-
borhoods in the Pittsburgh Area,* September 25, 1961, 5.

[47] (James V. Cunningham to author.) The Hyde Park-Kenwood project is
described in Julia Abrahamson, *A Neighborhood Finds Itself* (New York:
Harper and Brothers, 1959); Peter H. Rossi and Robert A. Dentler, *The
Politics of Urban Renewal: The Chicago Findings* (Glencoe, Illinois: Free
Press, 1961); James V. Cunningham, *The Resurgent Neighborhood* (Notre
Dame, Indiana: Fides Publishers, 1965).

the life of the citizen and city. In the tradition of Jacob Riis, the early social settlements, and Clarence Perry, Cunningham was an apostle of neighborhood as the source of cohesion and identity in the modern metropolis. "At stake" in neighborhood reconstruction, he insisted, was the "nature of urban life itself. Is there to be local community life, or only the big, impersonal mass of metropolis?" Attributes of a satisfactory neighborhood environment included necessary facilities and services, a sense of community, links to the broader metropolis, and diversity of population.[48]

Two ideals, not always compatible, were central to Cunningham's conception of neighborhood. He emphasized both cohesion and diversity as nuclear elements. "The present task," he argued, "is to build the district neighborhood well, to achieve in it the joint effort, the communication, the human attitudes of unity and responsibility which lead to a sense of community." But Cunningham also insisted that a "sense of community is an ingredient which only truly exists when it extends among and between all people—Negro and white, slow and brilliant, poor and wealthy."[49] Yet in Hyde Park-Kenwood, stabilization was achieved on the basis of creating an "interracial *middle-class* neighborhood" at the expense of lower-class whites and Negroes.[50] Similarly, sociologists like Herbert Gans suggest that similarities of age and class are closely correlated with ease and intensity of social interaction, that sharp differences in the age and class cycle can generate hostility and conflict.[51]

Along with visions of neighborhood cohesion and a ritualistic commitment to pluralism, Cunningham idealized the neighborhood as a source of participatory democracy. The "responsible citizen" was the "basic ingredient in neighborhood improvement. He is both the chief agent for achieving improvement and the

---

[48] *Ibid.*, 28, 40–41.

[49] *Ibid.*, 208, 209.

[50] Rossi and Dentler, *The Politics of Urban Renewal*, 52.

[51] Herbert J. Gans, *The Levittowners: How People Live and Politic in Suburbia* (New York: Pantheon Books, 1967), 170. Similarly, Rossi and Dentler find that in Hyde Park-Kenwood, "by and large, the local answer has been that integration cannot succeed unless the class level and customs of the two groups are approximately equal." (*The Politics of Urban Renewal*, 52.)

chief client to benefit from improvement. When the citizen plans and acts he becomes a man of dignity."[52] One might ask, however, whether the dignity and satisfaction inheres, in the long run, in the process of participation as opposed to the concrete material benefits that are the objective of social action.

Cunningham's zealous pursuit of the City of God ("the metropolis is a work of human art, and like every such work strives to capture God, to re-incarnate Him") contributed to tensions in the ACTION-Housing community organization program.[53] In one sense, ACTION-Housing was the most improbable agency to initiate and direct a movement for neighborhood self-assertion. It had been established in large degree to facilitate the civic coalition's renewal program. The community organization function placed ACTION-Housing in the awkward position of mediating between the neighborhood interests it helped arouse, on the one hand, and the political and business leadership upon whom it depended for support, on the other. The conflict was resolved, in part, by ACTION-Housing's tendency to work with a middle-class neighborhood clientele committed to stabilization rather than upheaval, and by a strong emphasis upon "self-help" rather than direct action.

A second source of tension evolved from the elitist and populist strains combined in ACTION-Housing. Even a radical democrat like Cunningham conceded the need for professional assistance to initiate and advise citizens' movements: "A key element . . . is this trained neighborhood professional. Probably no large urban effort can go far without his leadership."[54] The distinction, however, between democratic self-autonomy and external professional direction is often blurred. In the case of ACTION-Housing, the problem was especially acute. The agency's strength centered in its managerial and professional expertise. Although Cunningham's messianic zeal for citizen expression might have led him to equate anarchy with democracy at work, ACTION-Housing's executive was not inclined to do so. There existed, in essence, a conflict between the managerial, centralizing tendency

[52] Cunningham, *Resurgent Neighborhood*, 142; also Cunningham, "The Need for Neighborhood Power," *Pittsburgh Point*, June 20, 1968.
[53] Cunningham, *Resurgent Neighborhood*, 13.
[54] *Ibid.*, 142.

embodied in Loshbough, and the populist, decentralist values of Cunningham. The latter possessed an exceptional capacity to tolerate the frailties of mankind, but Loshbough did not tend to suffer fools gladly.

Cunningham's neighborhood ideals and Hyde Park-Kenwood experience, and Loshbough's interest in the concept and techniques of agricultural extension, did produce consensus on one point. Any ACTION-Housing experiment in community organization would revolve around the principle of self-help. Originally, emphasis fell upon minimizing federal assistance. According to ACTION-Housing in 1959, it was "neither possible nor desirable that all of our neighborhoods be renewed with Federal funds. Therefore, ACTION-Housing, Inc. has taken the initiative to assist the people to develop a new kind of self-help program. . . . This program would develop a series of neighborhood renewal projects, without Federal funds. Instead, it would utilize city and private resources to restore sound, but partially blighted neighborhoods."[55] Homewood-Brushton was selected in 1960 for the pilot program in urban extension.

A one-and-one-half square mile wedge jutting out from the eastern edge of Pittsburgh, Homewood-Brushton was divided by the Mainline of the Pennsylvania Railroad. The population, totaling approximately 30,000, was predominantly white south of the tracks, and Negro to the north. Annexed to Pittsburgh in 1868, Homewood-Brushton had been a fashionable residential community in the late nineteenth century; its residents included Carnegie, Frick, and Westinghouse. A more diversified growth area through World War I, the neighborhood suffered during the Depression from conversions of single family homes and deterioration of the housing stock. After World War II, the Negro population expanded rapidly, reaching tidelike proportions in the 1950's. The nonwhite population rose from 11 percent in 1930, 14 percent in 1940, and 22 percent in 1950 to 66 percent by 1960.[56]

---

[55] ACTION-Housing (Executive Director's) *Report to the Board of Directors and Members,* September 1959, 5.

[56] The growth of Homewood-Brushton is described in Delmar C. Seawright, "The Effect of City Growth on the Homewood-Brushton District of Pittsburgh," unpublished M.A., University of Pittsburgh, 1932; and Edward B.

Middle-class Negro homeowners, disturbed by the spread of blight and a growing crime problem, organized a Homewood Community Improvement Association in 1954. Its director, William Howell, went to see Loshbough soon after ACTION-Housing was established to discuss the possibility of assistance. ACTION-Housing always required this kind of formal neighborhood initiative before it would participate in neighborhood organization. The Homewood-Brushton Citizens Renewal Council was established in 1960 and ACTION-Housing received a $45,-000 grant from the Buhl Foundation to develop its experiment in self-help.[57]

The pilot demonstration in Homewood-Brushton operated on three fronts: citizen organization, preparation of a physical and social plan, and the expansion of municipal services and improvements. The results, in all three cases, were limited and ambiguous. Over a three-year period some 500 persons participated in the work of the Renewal Council. But, as ACTION-Housing conceded, the program reached "mainly the employed, stable, middle-income better educated people of the neighborhood. Only a handful of the thousands of unemployed, poverty-haunted, less stable, under-educated people of Homewood-Brushton have been involved."[58]

A great deal of effort was devoted to the preparation of a physical and a social plan. This did represent a new experience in neighborhood-centered planning, reminiscent of Hyde Park-Kenwood, but the results were not commensurate with the expectations. Although the physical plan was ready in 1961, widely discussed in the neighborhood through a number of "commu-

Olds, *Homewood-Brushton: A Pictorial Representation of its Growth, Population Characteristics, Housing Conditions, Health, Social Services, and Recreation Facilities* (Pittsburgh Federation of Social Agencies, Bureau of Social Research, n.d.).

[57] Also active in seeking assistance was the Homewood-Brushton Chamber of Commerce, and Mrs. Hannah Pearlman, a public assistance caseworker. On the origins of the Homewood-Brushton Citizens Renewal Council, see ACTION-Housing, *First Annual Report, Homewood-Brushton Self-Help Renewal Program, Covering Period from September 1, 1960 to August 31, 1961.*

[58] ACTION-Housing, *A Report on the Pilot Program for Neighborhood Urban Extension, Homewood-Brushton, 1960–1963,* 10.

nicators," extensively revised, and approved by both the City Planning Commission and City Council, it became a source of considerable frustration.[59] Residents were disappointed to find that public agencies did not invest the resources they had anticipated. As was suggested earlier, social action or the process of participation is not necessarily a substitute for concrete benefits. Its value is especially dubious if expectations are aroused and then thwarted. More generally, the Homewood-Brushton planning experience suggests there may be a discrepancy between the community organizer's ideals of intense citizen involvement, and the citizen's (especially lower class) emphasis upon visible, material improvement.

The Homewood-Brushton experiment did attempt, however, to benefit the neighborhood through a variety of small-scale material improvements. These included housing code compliance drives, new parking facilities, the organization of 4-H clubs, liquor license limitations, employment counseling, preschool classes, removal of abandoned cars, installation of mercury vapor lights, and increased street maintenance. On the other hand, little progress was made in dealing with what may have been the most important issue of all—"crime and the fear of crime."[60]

[59] The social plan encountered a variety of obstacles. In 1960–1961 part-time assistance was provided by the Health and Welfare Association, but the social plan made little progress and was not coordinated with the physical plan. At the end of the program year, the HWA assigned a full-time social planner. However, the Health and Welfare Federation and Citizens' Council clashed over program priorities, and it seemed that "the physical planners had much more confidence in sharing decision-making with citizens than the health and welfare planners, who in spite of their social worker backgrounds, seemed to be hesitant in working with citizens in an endeavor that involved exploring unfamiliar territory." Among the conclusions reached by ACTION-Housing, as a result of the physical and social planning process in Homewood-Brushton, was the difficulty in preparing a neighborhood plan in the absence of a city or metropolitan plan; the desirability of defining long-range neighborhood goals clearly in advance of planning; the need to prepare alternative proposals for consideration rather than single schemes; and the fact that both physical and social planning suffer when they do not proceed concurrently. ACTION-Housing, *Report on the Pilot Program* . . . , *1960–1963*, 15–19.

[60] One achievement in this area, as a result of neighborhood pressure, was the dismissal of the Pittsburgh Director of Public Safety (Kiernan Stenson to author).

Urban extension had barely been launched in Homewood-Brushton, and its implications absorbed, before ACTION-Housing began planning for a more elaborate demonstration. It sponsored a two-day Urban Extension Conference in July, 1961, attended by educators, social workers, and public officials from throughout the country. Here Cunningham defined the purpose of extension: "How to achieve mass participation, how to motivate people, how to give people the skills to make decisions, how to give them the help to unlock their potentialities." The nuclear principle was self-help; urban extension operated on the principle "that the best way to revitalize a neighborhood is to help its people achieve the desire and ability to help themselves." The origins of the extension idea and its techniques included "urban experience . . . community development programs abroad, and . . . the long and successful work of the Cooperative Extension Service in American rural areas."[61]

At the conference and in the application for funds to the Ford Foundation in the fall of 1961, ACTION-Housing placed great emphasis upon the potential contribution of the universities and the qualifications of the "extension worker, or urban generalist." The proposed demonstration would, presumably, "provide the prototype for linking the university to the urban neighborhood" through consultation, training programs, and research. The "urban generalist," described by Cunningham as the "key to the entire proposal," would function as the counterpart of the agricultural extension agent. He would develop the urban equivalents of agricultural extension: self-help; application of "advances in urban technology" in relation to family budgeting, nutrition, and child rearing; organization of an "educational system" to make this technology available; emphasis on youth development; and self-determination.[62]

Urban extension proved disappointing as far as delineating the role of the urban university was concerned. University participation by way of consultation, evaluation, and training was not only nominal, but the outgrowth of personal relationships rather

[61] ACTION-Housing, *Urban Extension*, 72; vi.
[62] ACTION-Housing, *Application for a Grant from the Ford Foundation*, 10; ACTION-Housing, *Urban Extension*, 72, 73.

than more formal institutional understandings.[63] The problem was similar to that described by Marris and Rein in their account of the community action programs sponsored by the Ford Foundation and President's Committee on Juvenile Delinquency. It centered on the conflict between operations and research. "If the research directors chafed," they explained, "at the inconsistency and incoherence of much that was done, the programme directors were equally impatient of pretentious methodology and theoretical preoccupations which failed to answer their needs."[64]

If urban extension did not succeed in clarifying the university's role in the urban sphere, neither did it produce an "urban generalist." The agricultural extension analogy, though plausible, was somewhat forced. Indeed, if one examines the qualities attributed to the generalist, he emerges as a kind of super social worker, an ideal-typical product of a community organization curriculum in a school of social work. As described by a Pittsgurgh social worker, the generalist was a person "steeped in city life," "knowledgeable about organized welfare resources," capable of exploiting them, at ease with the "lowest stratum" and "higher status groups," and "trained to compromise, negotiate and mediate between manifestly incompatible interests in an urban area."[65] Or, as ACTION-Housing described the attributes of this colossus: "thorough urban background; sensitivity; common sense; ability to learn rapidly; extensive interest; pioneer spirit; tenacity; team worker; intense dedication; maturity; empathy; organization experience; integrity; administrative ability; knowledge of planning, social welfare services, government; educational skills."[66] ACTION-Housing's first neighborhood urban extension worker, Kiernan Stenson, was, to be sure, well-informed, diligent, and effective in his pragmatic earthy fashion. But it would be more accurate to describe Stenson as a capable social work practitioner rather than the distinctive product of urban extension theory. The contribution of urban extension was

[63] Kiernan Stenson to author.
[64] Peter Marris and Martin Rein, *Dilemmas of Social Reform: Poverty and Community Action in the United States* (New York: Atherton, 1967), 200.
[65] ACTION-Housing, *Urban Extension*, 49–50.
[66] *Ibid.*, 100.

to provide a structure that enabled him to exercise his talents
—one that was more flexible than that of the old-line social
agencies.[67]

The Ford Foundation proved receptive to ACTION-Housing's
proposal. It had already initiated a grant program in 1959, which
enabled selected universities to experiment in urban extension;
and Paul Ylvisaker, director of the Public Affairs Division, was
familiar with the "successful application in Asia and other coun-
tries" of extension techniques.[68] The Foundation formally noti-
fied ACTION-Housing on January 12, 1962 that it had approved
a $325,000 grant; $75,000 would be supplied immediately for
planning, and the remainder would be contingent upon raising
a matching sum of $250,000.

In cooperation with the City Planning Department, and at the
request of local citizens, three neighborhoods were selected for
the five-year demonstration launched in 1963. Extension work in

[67] Efforts on the part of the neighborhood workers to live up to the urban
generalist ideal proved emotionally and physically exhausting. Cunningham
preferred to focus responsibility on a single individual on the grounds that
a staff or team effort would discourage citizen participation (Kiernan Stenson to author).

[68] Ford Foundation, *Urban Extension: A Report on Experimental Programs
Assisted by the Ford Foundation* (October 1966); ACTION-Housing,
Urban Extension, 4. Loshbough had been discussing with Ylvisaker the
possibility of a Ford grant to ACTION-Housing since 1960. Ultimately, the
Ford Foundation contributed a total of $475,000. Thirteen local foundations
and corporations contributed $404,000. Smaller contributions from the
City Planning Department ($50,000), Urban Redevelopment Authority
($40,000), Community Chest of Allegheny County ($4500), Department
of Labor ($39,500), and the Neighborhood Citizens Councils ($57,500)
raised the total to $1,070,500 for the five-year demonstration. (Statement
prepared for author by ACTION-Housing, June 1968.)

The Ford Foundation considered the ACTION-Housing extension program
as the most successful in the area of "direct neighborhood services," but
added that "while the Pittsburgh project has become something of a yard-
stick for efforts at community organization, it has still to work out a design
for university involvement which matches the expectations of the urban
extension concept" (Ford Foundation, *Urban Extension,* 35, 38). The Ford
grants for urban extension between 1959 and 1966 totaled $4.5 million.
Participating institutions, besides ACTION-Housing, included: University
of Wisconsin, Rutgers, University of Delaware, University of California
(Berkeley), University of Missouri, University of Oklahoma, Purdue, and
University of Illinois.

Homewood-Brushton continued. Hazelwood-Glenwood, the second neighborhood, was situated in the 15th ward, south of Schenley Park and fronting on the Monongahela River. Its environment was dominated by the Jones and Laughlin steel plants. A serious unemployment problem existed as a result, in part, of automation. The 1960 median family income of $5016 compared unfavorably with the city median of $5605. Some 24 percent of the housing units were classified as deteriorated or dilapidated. The neighborhood confronted a juvenile crime and school dropout problem (10 percent of the first four graduating classes in the senior high school entered college, compared to the city-wide average of 30 percent). Most important, perhaps, Hazelwood was a neighborhood in transition; its Negro population increased from 6 percent in 1940 to 11.4 percent in 1950 and 17 percent by 1960. As a result of physical deterioration and racial anxieties, the "neighborhood image" had changed within recent years: "ten years ago there was a pride in the neighborhood and the residents had a sense of status living in the community. . . ." Now pride was giving way "to discouragement and decline."[69]

ACTION-Housing had been involved with the third neighborhood, Perry Hilltop, since the late 1950's. Its 2546 acres sprawled across the East Central and North East sections of the North Side. Primarily a residential environment whose population totaled nearly 35,000, it suffered from incipient blight and racial tensions. A Perry Hilltop Action Committee had been organized in 1958 in response to pressure on school facilities created by North View Heights, a public housing project. The Committee soon broadened its scope and requested ACTION-Housing to prepare a community survey. ACTION-Housing's integrated Spring Hill Gardens apartments added to the anxieties of the white population.[70]

Operationally, urban extension was similar to the pilot demonstration in Homewood-Brushton. It focused upon citizen organization, physical and social planning, and neighborhood improvement. To some degree, however, community organization

---

[69] City of Pittsburgh, Department of City Planning, "Report on Selection of Three Neighborhood Urban Extension Communities," in ACTION-Housing, *A Plan of Operations for Neighborhood Urban Extension*, 60.

[70] *Ibid.*, 66ff; ACTION-Housing, *The Perry Hilltop Study*, 1961.

was stressed in Homewood-Brushton, education for "employment and human development" in Hazelwood, and public services in Perry Hilltop. Following the Economic Opportunity Act and establishment of the Mayor's Committee on Human Resources in 1964, ACTION-Housing under contract linked extension to the antipoverty program in Homewood-Brushton and Hazelwood, and in two additional neighborhoods—Lawrenceville and South Oakland.

According to ACTION-Housing, "any serious program of neighborhood vitalization encompasses not only housing, but the whole range of neighborhood life . . . and depends on creating in neighborhoods a sense of community as well as a citizenry that is effectively utilizing and integrating urban resources."[71] By this lofty test, urban extension could not be judged a success. As was suggested earlier, a great deal of frustration was generated in Homewood-Brushton because resources did not match expectations. Residents claimed "that there has been a continuing drag in allocating appropriate resources to the neighborhood, resulting in discouragement . . . and a growing trend towards militancy. Many Homewood residents were angry with fear that all of the carefully laid plans for an improved environment would not materialize."[72] Furthermore, the neighborhood extension workers found that the assignment of new resources, such as additional personnel from health or welfare agencies, was of limited value if the basic structure and allocation of services remained unchanged, and if the new resources were not coordinated with the ACTION-Housing program.[73]

In Hazelwood and Perry Hilltop, urban extension did not arrest deterioration of the "sense of community" resulting from

[71] ACTION-Housing, A Plan of Operations for Neighborhood Urban Extension, 7.

[72] ACTION-Housing, A Report on Neighborhood Urban Extension, The Fourth Year, 1966, 23. At a "Town Meeting" in Homewood-Brushton in December, 1967, attended by Mayor Joseph Barr, it was reported that "lack of decent housing was precisely what the . . . citizens had come to complain about—that and inadequate services and police protection. Taken together, their charges amount to this: they are not getting their share of the resources that are available." Funds had still not been allocated for the Homewood North Conservation project. Pittsburgh Point, December 21, 1967.

[73] Kiernan Stenson to author.

Low-cost housing, old and new: looking north from the Boulevard of the Allies with Terrace Village public housing in the background, 1951.

racial tensions. Perry Hilltop residents feared that the "neighborhood was becoming a poverty area, and perhaps a dumping ground for all relocation that has been and will be necessitated by massive Urban Renewal projects on the North Side." And in Hazelwood, where the Negro population doubled within ten years, " 'conservative,' old line white families, and large pockets of first and second generation white immigrants with strong ethnic traditions, have made assimilation most difficult. The gap between the Negro and white community has grown to the point where it is one of the most determinant factors in the neighborhood."[74]

Nothing could be more unrealistic, perhaps, than to evaluate the urban extension experiment in terms of its own objectives—neighborhood regeneration and cohesion rooted in a process of self-help and universal citizen participation. These implied a capacity to transcend the centrifugal pressures of modern urban life: heterogeneity; the diminished functional significance of neighborhood in light of modern transportation and communications technology; the dependence of the neighborhood upon external resources, city-wide and national; and possibly the indifference of most persons to a Cunningham-type activism compared to concrete material gain, however achieved.

On a less lofty plane, urban extension did have constructive implications. It was a kind of community organization laboratory, testing a wide range of programs and ideas, and a tribute to ACTION-Housing's experimental approach to housing and broader social problems. In Homewood-Brushton, for example, much was learned about the process of neighborhood-centered physical and social planning. The extension process led to numerous concrete neighborhood improvements. It marked the emergence of a new kind of community organization strategy, one that placed less emphasis than the Alinsky Industrial Areas Foundation upon conflict, but more emphasis upon citizen participation than the Ford Foundation community action programs of the early 1960's.[75] Urban extension and ACTION-Housing also played an important role in shaping the Pittsburgh anti-poverty program after 1964. Finally, urban extension marked a watershed in Pittsburgh history. Even though it did not reach and organize the poorest elements of the population, it did encourage the emergence of new neighborhood leaders and pro-

[74] ACTION-Housing, A Report on Neighborhood Urban Extension, The Fourth Year, 1966, 24.
[75] The Ford community action experiment is described in Marris and Rein, Dilemmas of Social Reform; and Ford Foundation, American Community Development: Preliminary Reports by Directors of Projects Assisted by the Ford Foundation in Four Cities and a State (March 1964).

vided many other citizens with some voice in decisions affecting their physical and social environment.[76] For all its limitations and contradictions, the extension process represented a sharp contrast to the historic tradition of elite initiative in defining issues and shaping the environment.

Still another challenge to this tradition was conspicuous by the late 1960's. It differed from urban extension in its "indigenous" origins, militancy, and emphasis upon lower-class involvement. Characteristic of the new type of leadership was William "Bouie" Hayden and the United Movement for Progress. A Homewood-Brushton black militant, Hayden described his organization as a movement "started at the grass roots, by the poor and for the poor. . . . Its primary power is people power. Even if it never receives a cent, the United Movement for Progress will build power to help people crash out of Nigger Hell."[77] Similarly, Homewood's Holy Cross Episcopal Church under Canon Junius Carter began working in 1968 toward a "united black community which . . . must have the major share of its economic, educational, law enforcement, recreational, and housing concerns controlled by its own black residents." Concrete programs included ownership and management of ACTION-Housing's Kelly-Hamilton rehabilitation project, efforts to establish a cooperative supermarket, and the organization of Forever Action Together—a federation of more than seventy black groups.[78]

[76] Meyer Schwartz, contrasting neighborhood citizen groups with agencies like the Allegheny Conference on Community Development, has emphasized the need for some mechanism to provide them with technical assistance. At a Conference on Urban Organizing held in Pittsburgh in the fall of 1967, he proposed the creation of a center to provide such expertise on behalf of "*variegated* relatively *independent,* indigenous *militant* organizations of the poor." It would, "upon request from indigenous organizations . . . set forth the alternative immediate objects and tactics linked to alternative long-term goals." Meyer Schwartz, "Point-Counterpoint in Urban Organizing" (unpublished paper, November 14, 1967).

[77] United Movement for Progress, *Mimeographed Fund Appeal,* February 1968. Still another source of citizen organization and advocacy that emerged in Homewood-Brushton in the late 1960's was "Forward Grass Roots," sponsored by the Catholic, Episcopal, and Presbyterian churches. This was the first such social action experiment by the Pittsburgh churches, who had consulted with Saul Alinsky (Kiernan Stenson to author).

[78] *Pittsburgh Point,* July 11, 1968. Carter had come to Pittsburgh from Elizabeth, New Jersey, and achieved prominence following the Martin

Thus the 1960's witnessed the emergence of a new neighborhood-centered quest for power whose long-term consequences cannot be predicted.[79]

Luther King riots in April, 1968. Assisting him in the organization of FAT was Nick Flournoy, a Homewood-Brushton organizer.

[79] For efforts to formulate a theory of neighborhood government, see Milton Kotler, "Two Essays on the Neighborhood Corporation," in *Urban America: Goals and Problems* (compiled and prepared for the Subcommittee on Urban Affairs of the Joint Economic Committee, Congress of the United States) (Washington, D.C., 1967), 170–191. Also, Richard F. Babcock and Fred P. Bosselman, "Citizen Participation: A Suburban Suggestion for the Central City," *Law and Contemporary Problems,* 32 (Spring 1967), 220–231.

ILLUSTRATION CREDITS

Index